PRAISE FOR CALL OF THE LARK

"**A poignantly honest, beautifully written account of one woman's journey to spiritual and emotional independence.** Whether describing the poverty of her childhood in rural Ireland, or the experience of immigration to America, or the discipline and turmoil she encountered in convent life, Mulligan vividly and flawlessly evokes the worlds she has traveled through. As truthfully as she is—as willing to confront moments of pain, confusion, and disappointment—Mulligan is utterly devoid of bitterness. Hers is a memoir to savor and remember."

> —**Peter Quinn**, American Book Award–winning author of *Banished Children of Eve* and *The Man Who Never Returned*

"**Maura Mulligan opens a dusty window on a number of worlds.** In clear, luminous prose, she tells a dry-eyed story of redemption that lifts both the heart and soul. An essential, revealing chapter in the Irish-American story."

> —**Larry Kirwan**, author of *Green Suede Shoes* and *Rockin' The Bronx*

Call of the Lark **gives the reader that rare gift that only truly imaginative writing can bestow: the sense** ⸺ **stepped live into another world.** Here we experience ⸺ ain of leaving behind parents and home, the confusing ⸺ a new country and the long journey embarked on. But ⸺ always looks out from behind the new, waiting to be re⸺ d. This is a story of emigration, of unshakeable loyaltie⸺ e never abandoned. A remarkable memoir."

> —**Kathleen Hill**, author of *Who Occ⸺ s House* and *Still Waters In Niger*

"**Maura Mulligan's journey is infused with the magic of dancing,** and a consistently playful and questioning spirit."

> —**Gemma Whelan**, author of *Fiona: Stolen Child*

"The voice of a character is the writer's gift to the reader. Here, we are embraced in a West of Ireland rhythm and cadence like that captured by Synge in 'The Playboy of the Western World' and 'Riders to the Sea'—an unforgettable book."

—**Dennis Smith**, author of *Report From Ground Zero* and
A Song For Mary

"A beautifully drawn and evocative memoir full of rich detail. *Call of the Lark* perfectly captures the unique atmosphere of rural Mayo. A wonderful read, and a great historical resource."

—**Kate Kerrigan**, author of *Ellis Island*

"Maura Mulligan's vivid memoir throws memorable light onto a hidden corner of life. This is a book about a woman's journey towards herself."

—**Belinda McKeon**, author of *Solace*

"In spite of the heartbreak, this book has lightness to it—a dancer's lightness."

—**Alphie McCourt**, author of *A Long Stone's Throw*

"A weaver of words, Maura Mulligan has created a textured snapshot of a changing world. She has skillfully woven together the frayed threads of painful memories, transforming the sights, sounds and smells of Aghamore through the lens of time and distance…always returning to what is 'real' within her."

—**Sheila A. McHugh**, chairperson, Achill Heinrich Böll Association

Helen
a very happy birthday
October 2012
with love
Angela

Call of the Lark

A MEMOIR

Call of the Lark
A MEMOIR

MAURA MULLIGAN

GREENPOINT PRESS
NEW YORK, NY

ISBN 978-0-9832370-5-1
Greenpoint Press,
a division of New York Writers Resources
P. O. Box 2062
Lenox Hill Station
New York, NY 10021

New York Writers Resources:
www.greenpointpress.org
www.newyorkwritersworkshop.com
www.ducts.org

Book Cover Designed by Eileen Connolly
Interior Book Designed by Robert L. Lascaro
www.lascarodesign.com
Typeset in Adobie Caslon
Display type: Zapfino
Printer: Lightning Source

Library of Congress Cataloging-in-Publication Data
Mulligan, Maura
Call of the Lark
ISBN 978-0-9832370-5-1

Printed in the United States of America
on acid-free paper

CONTENTS

For
MAG
You are missed

ACKNOWLEDGMENTS

*T*HIS BOOK WOULD NOT BE IN YOUR HANDS, had I not wandered into the Scoil Acla writers' week on Achill Island, County Mayo. It was there, in the silence of Sliabh Mór and the roar of the North Atlantic, that I heard the echoes of childhood mingle with the winds of emigration. *Míle buíochas* to poet and workshop leader, Macdara Woods. It was he who started me off on this journey of memories.

I owe gratitude also to Heinrich Böll Association. It was during my residency at the Böll Cottage that I finished this book.

I am grateful to the many supporters of the Scoil Acla writing workshop who always welcome me back to Achill. Your continuous presence at the readings in Ted Lavelle's inspired me to keep going with the project. Thank you to: Marie-Louise Colbert, Nora & Joe Daly, Mairéad & Paddy Lineen, Sheila McHugh, John McHugh, John "Twin" and Mary McNamarra, the O' Leary family from Cork and the many others who, year after year, cheered the work-in-progress.

Míle buíochas also to the regulars, the participants who joined me at the Scoil Acla workshop and constantly reminded me that it was time to get this book into the hands of readers: Marie Clynes, Ethna Johnston, Tessa Johnston, Aibhlín, Aodan & Eamonn O' Leary and Anne Shannon.

To Seán, Áine, Mary, Michael and Claire Charleton, Patricia & Séamus Conboy, Terence & Gerardine Flanagan, and Máiread O' Donohue. Thank you for your care and generosity during my visits to Clare, Dublin, Galway and Mayo.

Thanks to Charles Hale, who, along with Malachy McCourt, founded the Irish American Writers & Artists salon (IAW&A). At these gatherings, I have enjoyed sharing some of these pages in an atmosphere of collegiality and support.

To my cheerleaders in New York, who kept yelling for me to finish, or showed up at readings to cheer me on: Deirdre Batson, David Carey, Michele Cetera, Pat Daly, Sheila Fee, Martin Fitzpatrick, Corina Galvin, John and Ann Garvey, Sister Cecelia Hall, Dan Higgins, Marie Hudak, Martha Lahn, Barbara Lavinson, Peggy Logan, Mary Louise McCall, Patricia McEntegart, Doris Meyer, Pat McGivern, Sally Renda, Eileen Rowland Sheets, Todd Sassaman, Patrick Shalhoub and Arnene Weiss. Thank you all for your friendship and support.

Karen Daly, thank you for your professional encouragement, support and friendship.

Vera Johannessen, míle buíochas for the joyful reminders about our early dance years at the McNiff School, and for sharing your artistic space.

Tessa Johnston, you read drafts of early pages and encouraged me to continue. Thank you, Tessa, for your time and generosity.

Editor Vinnie Kinsella, my thanks to you for your sensitivity and honesty.

Honor Molloy, tale spinner and IAW&A member, thanks for introducing me to my cover designer, Eileen Connelly.

Book designer, Bob Lascaro, thank you for bringing this book to life. Thank you to Gini Kopecky Wallace for your professional attitude and meticulous attention to detail.

LeeAnn Pemberton, for your support, as well as your professional encouragement and brainstorming through the title changes, go *raibh maith agat!*

Pat Phelan, I am grateful for your professional encouragement and suggestions.

Gerry Regan, thank you for the shout-out on wildgeese.com

Anne Shannon, it was in your charming home, sitting by the fire, that some of these pages came to life. Thank you, Anne, for your friendship and support.

Dennis Smith, you sent accolades on early pages and encouraged me to include additional childhood memories. Thank you.

My confidence as a writer grew when Joe Byrne published my work in *Glór Achadh Mór*; John Garvey, in the newsletters of the Mayo Society of New York and the American Irish Teachers' Association; Patricia Harty, in *Irish America*; Jonathan Kravetz, in the literary webzine Ducts.org; Bill Lynch, in *Set Dancing News*; Ray O' Hanlon, in *The Irish Echo,* and Marc-Yves Tumin and Paddy McCarthy, in the *Irish Examiner*.

To teacher/editor Charles Salzberg: in your class some of these pages were critiqued. Thank you for your commitment to this book. May you and Greenpoint Press have continued success.

And now, it must be said that I could not have written this book without the help, encouragement and undying support of my New York writers' group: Diana Kash, David Perez, Dan Rous, Ellen Schecter and the late, dear, Hilda Meltzer. You patiently read draft after draft, told me to put back those bits I took out and, to top it all off, you rescued the missing commas. I thank you for your time, inspiration, creativity, honesty and friendship. I wish you much success with your own books. May you be forever blessed.

Nieces Caroline, Susan, Denise and Shannon, thank you for the joyful hugs of love and support from London.

And, finally, to my sister, Bridie, and brother, John, who couldn't wait for me to finish, and then applauded loudly when I wrote the last word. Thank you for believing in me.

I love you always.

FOREWORD

I FIRST MET MAURA MULLIGAN back in the nineties, on the impossibly beautiful Achill Island, which juts out into the North Atlantic from the coast of Mayo. It was a morning at the end of July and a group of us were sitting in the main classroom of Bunacurry School engaged in a writing workshop as part of the Achill traditional music and dancing summer school, Scoil Acla.

Business had already begun for the day when a self-contained red-haired woman, straight backed and light on her feet, came in and explained that she had arrived for the dancing, but was a week too early, and would we mind if she sat in with us to see what we were at. Although, she added, she had never set about "creative writing" in her life.

What should I do, she said, where should I begin? So I suggested she go and sit somewhere on the island, alone, and listen. To what, she asked. Just listen, I said. Don't try to hear anything, or to think, just listen and it will happen.

And she did, and it did, and that's how the writing started.

But, of course, the truth is that she had always been a listener, and an observer, as immediately became clear. She is a storyteller, Burns' chiel amang ye takin' notes, a dancer who danced also with words and images, and a world of memories. She was, so to speak, a writer waiting to happen: a writer before she wrote a line.

With a story to tell that is a whole collection of stories, each one inside another like Russian dolls, a story of several lives, unfolding each one to become the next in turn.

They say that writers are people for whom writing is more

difficult than it is for other people. I believe there is a lot of truth in that. And the easier it looks on the page, the harder it has been getting it there. Maura has worked hard on this one, in the living of it and the writing of it. And here it is. Arrived.

As I always knew it would, from the time I read a piece of hers with the question posed to her by one of her quintessentially urban students in New York: what is a geese, Miss? Only writers get asked questions like that, and hear them, and then spend a lifetime answering them. What is a geese, Miss? What is it not?

Macdara Woods
DECEMBER 2011

Author's Note

The people, places and situations in this memoir are real.
I reconstructed the dialogue as best I can remember it.
I have changed some names because I am sensitive
to the right of privacy.

CHAPTER 1

SMOKE ASCENDING

O UR LACED-UP, LOW-HEELED SHOES, not yet broken in, clip-clopped on the cobblestone pavement as we lined up two by two. A funeral was a solemn event. This was our first as postulants. We wore long black cloaks over black pleated skirts that reached our ankles. We tried not to stare at each other in the unfamiliar garb as we lit our candles for the procession.

Twice the wind caused me to nudge Brigid, the postulant beside me, for another light. Mother Mistress, the nun in charge of postulants and novices, would surely have something to say on the following day about postulants not being able to follow directions at a funeral procession. Her aim was to mold us into perfect nuns, so conformity was of the utmost importance.

"The exterior reflects the interior, Sisters," she would say. "If you are to develop strong spiritual lives, you must be in command of your external movements at all times. Custody of the eyes, Sisters. That's what's important."

Mariella, the novitiate equivalent of a class clown, would mimic Mother Mistress and point a finger at one or another of us if she noticed any infraction of the novitiate rules. On this occasion, the cloaks brought on such an image that Mariella was unable to control a fit of laughter. She spun her plump body around and faced the line of postulants.

"Egads," she said with great amusement in her bright, brown eyes. "We look like a buncha witches."

Our shoulders shook with repressed giggles as Mother Mistress quickly made her way in our direction. A tall nun, her graceful, stately walk gave her the appearance of floating above ground. Her stern, ageless face was visible only from her thin eyebrows to her chin. A black veil floated behind her.

She wagged a long finger at Mariella. "You, Sister, and all of you—" she lowered her glasses over her long nose, the better to stab us with her sharp look. "You must learn to practice custody of the eyes. You are not, after all, lining up for the Miss America Pageant."

There were stifled giggles behind cupped hands. Although I was twenty-one, a little older than most, I was new to some aspects of American life. I had never heard of the Miss America Pageant.

I tried to focus on the candle in my right hand and the Latin prayer book in my left hand while the sound of the death bell filled my ears. We began our chant, *De Profundus clam ad te Domine.*

But I was not crying out to the Lord from the depths. During the chant, it was my grandmother's funeral in Ireland, not the one I was attending, that commanded my presence.

My mother and her sister, Annie, were pouring cups of tea and glasses of port wine while they argued about the funeral arrangements. Their angry whispers were getting louder. Neighbors sat around the kitchen fire in high-backed wooden chairs telling stories about ghosts rising from the dead. They drank mugs of black stuff called porter from a barrel. To me, at age four, it smelled like the water near the ditch in the Well Field where frogs laid their eggs.

Men took off their caps as they came in the door, the taller ones hunching down, minding their heads. The older women in their long, black skirts and laced-up boots would kneel to say a prayer and then take one of the clay pipes with tobacco that lay at the foot of the coffin. They admired my grandmother's repose.

"She looks grand. God rest her."

"Oh, aye, a fine corpse. God rest her soul."

I asked my grandfather why they were all smoking pipes.

"The smoke from the pipes means your grandma's soul is going up to Heaven," he said as he sat looking into the fire.

The women moved in closer to the hearth, lowering their shawls to show long gray hair tightly plaited and twisted into a knot at the nape. There was talk about the price of eggs, the rain, and the Yanks that came home to visit from New York and Boston. Then a hush fell as someone mentioned the priest's announcement about the new graveyard that was to be opened. The next person to die in the parish of Aghamore will be its first occupant, he had said.

"I wish someone else in the parish went first," my mother complained.

"It's not right for her to be there by herself when all belonging to her are in the old graveyard," Aunt Annie said.

"Sure we all know that. But someone has to start off the new one, and you know very well you can't go against the priest's wishes," my mother insisted.

"Priest or no priest, believe you me, I'll put a stop to it."

"Well thanks and glory be to God, that's a terrible thing to say. Don't let the neighbors hear you."

"She'll have a place of honor, surely, being the first in the new graveyard," said Kate Snee, who had her own clay pipe that she brought to all the wakes and smoked every day in the comfort of her own kitchen.

"It'll be awful lonesome for her there with no one but herself, I'm thinking," said Anne Burke, the only old woman at the wake with a short haircut. Her big hand stroked the few hairs she had growing on her chin. I thought she looked more like my grandfather than my grandmother.

Aunt Annie put down the teapot and glared at the two women. Anne Burke looked away. She took a piece of newspaper, twisted it into a rope, and stuck it into the fire to get another light for her pipe.

Kate said the arthritis was "a divil of a thing." When she dropped her pipe, I picked it up and handed it back to her. In response, she gave me a penny for being good. When my younger sister Mag saw the penny, she wanted it. I had to kick her in the shins to make her mind her own business. Her screams caused my mother to grab both of us by our collars. She spoke to us under her breath.

"Will ye give over, for the love a God and the night that's in it? Isn't your grandmother stretched out there in her coffin lookin' at ye?"

"There's no more ham," my cousin Nuala whispered in Mam's ear, causing her to let go of Mag and me.

"That the divil may fire the poverty anyhow," she mumbled, looking at the now empty mugs and plates on the table. "I wish your father didn't have to work beyond in England."

The house was gray with smoke as everyone, men and women, sent my grandmother to Heaven in winding curling clouds. When the wind blew down the chimney, the smoke from the turf blew all over us in the kitchen, making me cough. Mam took the tongs and fixed the coals and sods of turf. Aunt Annie followed her to the fire because she had more to say.

"To the divil with the priest. She's not staying in that new graveyard by herself, and I'll see to that!"

Mam put the tongs back on the hob.

"I'm washing my hands of this carry-on, so I am. 'Tis a sacrilege, the way you're talking," she said. "If you don't pipe down and give over, I'm not speaking to you again."

The night following the burial in the new graveyard, Aunt Annie waited for the sun to sink behind the haunted house that was next to our Well Field—just beyond the gooseberry and black current bushes. She cornered her husband, Pat, and his cousin, Tom Mick, as they returned from the cow-house.

"Let ye go, the two a ye, and dig her up."

"Dig her up?" Pat was horrified. He dropped the bucket of milk he was carrying in, its creamy whiteness turning brown as it ran down the street.

"Aye, dig her up, I'm telling you. And put her to rest where she belongs, with the rest of her relations by the stone wall with the round hole where the horn of gold was found."

"Leave her be. 'Tis wrong, I'm saying, to be meddling with sacred ground. You won't have a day's luck if you put a shovel to that ground," my grandfather said.

When I asked about the horn of gold, my mother said it was time for the likes of me to go to bed. My grandfather told me not to cry, that he'd tell me the story about the magic horn of gold the banshee left in the wall over my great grandparents' grave a hundred years ago, at a time when the people were starving with the hunger.

It was difficult to listen to the story with all the noise. My mother was trying to stop them from going to dig up my grandmother. Aunt Annie was pushing the two men out the door. Not only that, she was going along with them to make sure the proceedings went right.

So, when the moon was high over the top of Croagh Patrick, Aunt Annie and the two men in Wellingtons and topcoats went out in the cold wet night to dig up my grandmother.

"I wouldn't go within an ass's bray of a graveyard in the middle of the night, much less dig up the dead," Mam said. Then she added, "May they rest in peace."

After the deed was done, they carried Grandmother's body over the narrow iron gate and buried her beside the stonewall in the old graveyard.

"Oh, the Lord save us," my mother said. "If anyone finds out, we'll be the talk of the parish."

For several years afterwards, the two sisters ignored each other.

Silence. The chanting stopped. I heard the Sisters' beads jingling against the polished wooden benches. During that "Office of the Dead," my mind had wandered back fifteen years. What bounced me back to the present was when we began praying for the success of President Kennedy and for the repose of the souls of those who were shot during the riot in Mississippi. ❧

CHAPTER 2

INSTRUCTIONS

HE DAY FOLLOWING THE NUN'S FUNERAL, Mother Mistress greeted us with the customary salutation, "Praised be Jesus Christ," as she hurried into the classroom with her usual sense of urgency. We stood at our desks to give the response in unison: "Forever be praised." Together we made the sign of the cross and recited the Lord's Prayer. That was the spiritual part of the daily ritual called "instructions."

During instructions, Mother Mistress would counsel us to walk gracefully, speak in low tones, and be meticulous in keeping the novitiate rules. "You must forget yourselves, Sisters, and think as members of the Franciscan family, where we are all one in the Lord," Mother Mistress would say. It was strange at first referring to personal belongings as "ours" instead of "mine." When I had to admit I couldn't find "our" toothbrush and that I needed another, I giggled. Mother Mistress corrected me for two faults: misplacing property that belonged to the community and lacking the humility to take this matter seriously. I pulled myself together and tried to feel guilty. But in spite of my best efforts, I still thought it was funny.

Once in a while, we'd find her in a good mood. On those occasions, instead of pointing out how we should conduct ourselves, she told us stories about the lives of senior Sisters who were on missions in places like Bolivia, where they traveled around on the backs of mules as they went about their work helping the poor. Those were times when I wanted to share my own experiences about growing up in Mayo, when small farmers still used horses to pull a plough and harrow.

In early spring when the crocus, blackthorn sloe, daffodils and bluebells began to color the fields and hedges, my mother would cut potato slits sitting on a stool in the middle of the kitchen floor with a big *ciseán* of spuds at her feet. On her right-hand side was a bucket to hold the slits. She took one potato at a time, turned it a few times in her fingers and sliced it just right with the sharp knife. She cut the potato between two eyes, leaving one eye on each half.

"These are the sprouts of the potato, and if the bit sowed has no eye, there won't be any spud," she told us.

While my mother slit the spuds, my father put holes with a dibble in the newly plowed ridges. Mag and I carried tin cans full of slits. I took one side of the ridge, and Mag took the other. The fun began for me when Mag was trying to catch up. If I was way ahead on my side of the ridge, I'd show off by juggling the slits—throwing them up in the air and trying to catch them again.

"Let ye stop the tomfoolery and not miss any holes," my father said wiping the sweat off his forehead with the sleeve of his gray flannel shirt. Like other small farmers during the forties and fifties, he got ready for his trips to England every March. Grandfather helped him after the sowing of the potatoes, and again when the stalks were out of the ground. When white blossoms covered the black soil, I knew it was almost time for Dad to leave and do this same work in some much bigger farm in England.

"As soon as I'm done with the second spraying, 'twill be time for me to be off," he said.

The spraying machine was like a small barrel with a hose on the side. After he filled it with a solution of bluestone and washing soda that he mixed together, he strapped the machine to his back and walked up and down the field spraying every stalk in sight.

"The machine on your back is a great invention altogether," Grandfather said. "Sure in my own day, the spraying was done from a bucket you had to keep filling every five minutes." He puffed on his pipe and spat on the ground from the side of his mouth before he continued. "And I mind dipping a twig brush into the bucket and spraying it over the potato stalks. Ah, but I'll keep an eye on the weather after you leave anyhow," he added.

Grandfather reminded us that we were lucky we weren't alive a hundred years earlier, in the dread of "Black 47," when the potatoes rotted in the ground.

"Why did they rot?" I asked him.

"We'll say no more" was what he always said.

I would share some of these childhood experiences with my novitiate friends Brigid, Louisa and some others at recreation. They were enthralled to hear how in winter, we gathered in the neighbor's house to listen to radio programs and sing along with Gogi Grant when he brought "The Wayward Wind" to our ears all the way from America. But, as always, sharing personal experiences was not allowed in the novitiate. In order to gain holiness, we were supposed to forget the past and free our minds to be one with the Lord.

On this day, Mother Mistress started out by saying, "Do not draw attention to yourselves or distract other Sisters. Be still and allow the workings of the Holy Spirit to direct your lives."

She glared at Mariella and waited for what seemed forever before she spoke again. "Sister Mariella!" she said finally, pronouncing her name with such emphasis you'd think the poor girl was in some great danger. We all tried to avert our eyes as Mariella got on her knees to take her correction.

"Sister Mariella, I could not believe my ears yesterday at Sister Mary Frances' funeral. What *were* you thinking, Sister?"

A good thing it's not me on my knees, I thought. I might have felt obliged to tell her about my grandmother's wake.

Mariella looked up from her pose of submission and said with a straight face, "Sorry, Mother. I couldn't help it. We did kinda look like…a buncha witches with those black cloaks and all."

When she saw that the rest of us had trouble hiding our giggles, Mariella burst out laughing.

"You have much to worry about. You *must* mature if you are going to persevere in the religious life," Mother Mistress said with anger in her voice. I was sure I wasn't the only one thinking that if this is the way to gain holiness, acquiring it wasn't going to be easy.

The icy blue eyes next shifted in my direction.

"And you, Sister Maura. You hold your head to the left side. Do not walk alongside Sister Louisa, who holds her head to the right. Together you look like a set of bookends walking into chapel. Remember, the senior Sisters cannot be distracted by such ungraceful behavior."

"Ungraceful behavior!" I wanted to shout. "Don't you know I'm a dancer? It was in my resume under hobbies, or activities of interest or something." But I knew that all our accomplishments prior to entering religious life didn't matter now. I was expected to forget the past, to strive to be a new woman, worthy of the title "Bride of Christ."

"Yes, Mother," was all I said. ⮧

CHAPTER 3

THE CALL

ECAUSE OF MY LOVE OF IRISH DANCING, I gave it up a year before entering the convent. I decided that if it were too painful to live without dancing, that meant I didn't have "the call." It was a great gift to be called. Everyone said so—especially my mother.

"You won't have a care in the world if you're married to the Lord," she always said.

On entrance day I chatted with Louisa in the meeting room known as Sacred Heart Hall, where we all assembled before closing the door to the world. Louisa, a petite Bostonian with a pretty face and large brown eyes, told us how sad she had been since her father died the year before and how peaceful she now felt when she realized that God had called her to religious life.

"What exactly did you feel was the call?" I asked her. She wasn't sure. "Just a desire to serve God," she said.

Brigid, a tall, thin, blond, fair-skinned girl with doll-like features and a bubbly personality, joined us.

"You sound Irish," she beamed.

"Yes, I am. Mayo. That's where I'm from. It's in the west."

"I've heard of Achill in Mayo. It's supposed to be beautiful."

"It is. I'm from a place called Aghamore. It's almost as picturesque as Achill," I lied.

"Well, listen, the next visiting day, you absolutely must meet my mother. She's from Derry."

"There are a few of us Irish here," Louisa chimed.

Brigid, Louisa, and some of the others called themselves Irish. But because they were born in the States, they were Americans to me. Beatrice and Mariella said they were Italian, even though it was their parents or grandparents who were from Italy. They were from Philadelphia. I knew that my accent stood out. I got embarrassed when they'd say, "That sounds so cute. Say it again."

Some of the girls who made up my "band" had completed college courses. A few had degrees. I didn't even know what the inside of a high school looked like. In the fifties, secondary education in Ireland was not free unless you had a scholarship. Still, my lack of formal education at twenty-one didn't keep me from considering myself more mature than some of the others.

I told them how my sister Mag, who was a year younger than me, had entered the order two years earlier, and how we were always in competition as children. Now, I was all too aware that Mag was called to a higher life before I was. I tried not to think about it because envy was one of the seven deadly sins.

"Since you have a sister in this order, you must know the scoop," Brigid beamed. "I mean you must know more about the happenings in the novitiate than the rest of us. Tell, tell." She lifted her eyebrows and opened her eyes wide in anticipation of news, or maybe gossip.

"I don't know anything more than you. Mag is kind of...aloof since she entered."

It was true. As soon as Mag arrived in New York, she got a job as a priest's housekeeper. Within a month, she decided to enter the convent. I was shocked, then jealous, and then tried to talk her out of going.

"You're only after coming here. Why are you doing this?"

"I'm called. I was at a retreat in the parish where I met the Franciscans. They do good work, taking care of kids from broken homes. I want to help them."

"But you haven't seen New York yet. You haven't gone dancing. Come with me to my dance class. Give yourself more time."

But Mag was set to go, and I felt resentful that she was called to a higher life.

"You know how it is," Louisa said. "When sisters are close in age. There's always jealousy."

"Yes," I said. "She probably thinks she's more advanced than me because she's two years ahead. Oops! I shouldn't think that way now."

"Oh, but you and your sister are so brave to come to a new country and then enter a religious order," Brigid remarked.

"My mother is going around telling all her friends about her daughter the nun," Louisa laughed.

"Still, some parents were upset on entrance day," I recalled.

"Maybe their daughters were only children and they wanted grandchildren?" Brigid offered.

"Well," I said, "if my mother were here, she would have told them to pipe down and stop their crying. One of her favorite sayings was, 'I wouldn't have a care in the world if I only had a bit of sense and married the Lord instead of your father.'"

They all laughed so loud Mother Mistress looked up from her knitting.

"When I came to America four years ago, all I thought about was dancing and marrying a handsome man," I said with a giggle, looking nervously in Mother Mistress's direction.

"She's not listening," said Brigid. "What made you change your mind?"

"The Call," exclaimed Beatrice, who had just joined our circle. She glanced here and there as if she were looking for someone or something. "How in the world do you explain it to people who don't understand or experience it?"

"I mean, it's not that you have a vision or anything," Louisa added. "It's just that you feel it's the right thing to do, like people who go into the Peace Corps."

"I didn't always want to be a nun," Brigid admitted. "But then the guys I was meeting weren't…well…worthy of me. So, here I am."

Brigid's remark made me think of Brian. But of course, it was against the rules to talk about former boyfriends.

Uncle Pake, who paid my passage to America, caught Brian and me kissing in the kitchen. When Brian had taken me home after a dance at City Center Ballroom, I invited him in for a cup of tea. Uncle Pake, a recovering alcoholic, walked in on our kiss after returning home from a meeting. He asked no questions when he threw Brian out.

"'Tis time for you to be off now so it is. This lass has to be up for work in the morning."

With that, he held open the door, and Brian walked off into the night. My Uncle did not speak of the incident except to say that he hoped it wasn't because of "the kiss in the kitchen," that I decided to leave the world behind.

"The ghosts of Pop's own life interfere with his good judgment," Cousin Nuala said. She was referring to the Great Depression of 1932.

When the Depression hit, her mother left her drunken husband in New York and somehow found her way to a boat and Ireland. Her belly big with Nuala waiting to be born, she checked into The Coombe hospital in Dublin, where she died in childbirth. My own mother raised baby Nuala until she was old enough to join Uncle Pake, her father, and her older sister, Mary, in New York.

That night of the kiss in the kitchen, Brian said, "You, you're too pretty to go into a convent." He took my hand and lifted it to his lips. I loved this romantic gesture, but this time, I took my hand away, "Brian, I feel called."

"Called? Why the hell are so many pretty girls going off to join the nuns? What a waste!"

I was never sure if I had the real call but figured I'd find out as I went along. I knew for sure that I didn't want a husband like Josephine's, Cousin Nuala's friend who lived next door. When I'd visit Josephine with Cousin Nuala, he'd try to "tickle" me when the two women weren't in sight. I once yelled at him to take his dirty paws off me, and he slunk off to the fridge for another beer. I felt I had put him in his place, but was leery of him ever after. Nuala told me that when he'd come home late, his red eyes would flash wildly if his dinner wasn't on the table waiting for him. He would beat Josephine when he was drunk. "I feel sorry for poor Josephine. She gets more than her fair share of black eyes from that bastard," Nuala added.

Since instructions were not a means of learning about spiritual matters, I decided that God must want me to attain such knowledge by myself. But how? Although I enjoyed learning the Latin psalms and chanting them, I could not fathom meditation. That skill was a complete enigma. It was taken for granted that we knew how to meditate, or that we would figure it out by ourselves. The spiritual reading during meals was meant to help us, but I couldn't focus on the message because I was always listening to how words were pronounced by the novices from the Bronx or Philadelphia.

We were each given a copy of *The Following of Christ* as well as other spiritual reading books for meditation. I tried imagining myself with the crowd as Jesus fed the poor with loaves and fishes. But the scene in my head switched from Judea to Mayo, where my younger brothers P.J. and Tommie were fishing in the Glór River, fighting over the catch of the day.

"He's mine. I saw him first."

"Feck off, will ya? I caught the bastard."

I saw my father taking off his belt and lashing out at both of them. Sometimes it was my mother reaching up over the fireplace to get the rod from its spot behind the bag of sugar on the mantelpiece. I saw myself, standing in front of Tommie to protect him from blows on the head, shoulders and legs—giving him a chance to run away from the wrath of her anger and hide under the table. I saw her throw down the rod when I tried to comfort Tommie, giving him bread and jam. I refused to talk to her.

Why won't these scenes stop? I asked myself. Still, I pondered, sending my thoughts in a purer direction, it must be God's will for me to put up with this if it's to bring holiness and peace. I admired the novices in chapel. They looked as if they knew how to meditate. There they were, sitting serenely, eyes closed and hands folded on laps. Surely, I thought, they must be in communion with God. Mother Mistress often reminded us of the difference between the postulants and novices.

"You postulants are still worldly. Some of you drove cars, planes and boats before coming here. But the novices, now they are forgetting about worldliness."

At times I worried that I was the only one who didn't know how to meditate. Then I'd hear one of the others flipping through the pages of *The Life of St. Francis* or some other book and I knew she didn't know either—a momentary consolation. Once I tried meditating on being present on the boat with Jesus when he calmed the storm. I could feel the storm rage and see His outstretched hand calming the surging waves. A pleasant, peaceful feeling followed. I thought I had mastered the technique. But then I'd fall into the sea. Knowing that I couldn't swim meant that I'd have to have faith that Jesus would save me. That scene always ended in a panic and the knowledge that I did not have that faith to believe I'd be saved from drowning.

Other meditation periods would find me in Ireland, lying in the back garden and watching the lark soar from a hawthorn bush near the stonewall. I knew it was my lark because it seemed always to wait for me to come into the garden before its song soared high into the clouds. I could hear it singing even when it was no longer visible. It lost itself in the evening sky where crimson and blue met the white clouds that floated downward to meet the purple heather.

There in the convent chapel, my mind saw the lark fly high above the stained glass windows, onto the choir loft. But now, instead of the joyous notes I remembered, its song seemed a screeching shrill as it flapped its wings in an attempt to fly through multicolored glass. ༀ

Mayo, Ireland
1930s–1950s

THE WAY HOME: This sign on the N17 road between Kilkelly and Knock points to our parish church and graveyard.

GRANDFATHER & GRANDMOTHER: Mary Anne and Thomas Connell take a rest after raking the hay. I think this photo is from the late 1930s. It's older than I am.

CHILDHOOD DAYS: Bridie on Mam's lap. I'm the one holding the puppy.

THE MULLIGAN FAMILY: This family photo was taken just before I left for America. Back: Maura, Dad, Bridie, Mam, and Mag. Front: Tommie, John, and P.J.

DANCING TEACHER, SÉAMUS FORDE: In my opinion, a pair of hornpipe shoes was the best going-away gift a dancer could receive from her teacher.

WHEN SÉAMUS FORDE VISITED NEW YORK:
Forty years later, we danced a step together.

CHAPTER 4

AN IRISH ACCENT

*M*OTHER MISTRESS ASSIGNED US as charges to some of the senior Sisters to help us learn about the work of the community.

"Sister Maura, you will not work with the children," she commanded. "You have an Irish accent, and I doubt if they would understand you. If the children can't understand you, they won't mind you. I think the best assignment for you is Sister Malachy's kitchen and the priests' house."

Sister Malachy was the priests' housekeeper. That meant I would be cleaning the priests' kitchen and helping with the cooking.

"The children are placed in our care," Mother Mistress explained, "until such a time as a foster home has been found or the court system decides that they should be returned to their families. Those of you who will be assisting the group mothers— the Sisters in charge of the children—are to report to work across the street in the boys' or girls' houses after breakfast. Go through Sacred Heart Hall and down the front steps. It should take you no more than five minutes to be on duty." That's what working with the children was called: duty.

My heart fell. I wanted to work with the children, play games with them and teach them to dance. I felt like telling this woman, whom

God had sent to direct my new life, that bosses at the New York Telephone Company where I worked my first four years in America were well pleased with my Irish accent. I was nominated for Miss Voice and Courtesy Award two years in a row, for God's sake.

I decided this must be a trial from God, such as St. Francis had. So I made up my mind to accept the assignment without thinking too much about it. But when we went to chapel to pray for guidance in the carrying out of our assignments, I was unable to pray. I found myself instead remembering my previous work as a housekeeper.

I was fourteen, the eldest of six, when word got around that the Flynns needed a maid to work in their posh house. Although my mother didn't exactly say it was time for me to leave our crowded house, she did say that working in a fine house like the Flynns' would improve my chances in America. My sisters, Mag, who was thirteen, and Bridie, twelve, would be glad to have a bit more space in the hag, our settle bed in the kitchen. P.J. and Tommie, who were six and eight, shared a bed my father made out of bits of timber. When my grandfather died, they moved out of my parents' room into his. My youngest brother, John, two at the time, slept in a cot at the head of my parents' bed.

In a big house like the Flynns', I'd have my own room. I'd have a real mattress, too. "Damn and blast the poverty. It won't be a mattress made out of canvas bags sewn together and filled with straw like what you're used to," Mam said. I'd learn how to set a table with china, even if I didn't know what china looked like. Mrs. Flynn would teach me which side of the plate the fork went and how to fold a table napkin, whatever that was. I'd learn how to put lunch on the table for Garda Flynn when he came home from the police station after a hard morning collecting fines for offenses like catching salmon in the off season and cycling on the road at night without a flashlight.

For weeks, I looked forward to my new adventure. But as the time to leave got closer, I had more spats than usual with Mag.

"I won't have to share that oul bed with you anymore," I said.

"I'll have a lovely room to myself."

"You're only going to be a maid, and you'll have a lot of hard jobs to do."

"Sure there won't be much to do in a grand house the like o' that," Mam said. I noticed a hint of doubt in her voice when she looked out the window, her eyes staring into space.

When it was time to go, I wanted to wear lipstick because that would mean I was grown up, but everyone knew that fourteen was too young for lipstick.

"Well, in the name of God, what the divil would the likes of us be doing with lipstick? Isn't it far from paint and powder we were reared!" my mother said.

As she helped me close the old gray cardboard suitcase that my father had used for his seasonal jobs in England, she asked me, "What way are you, *A Ghrá*?" I didn't answer. I froze hearing the term of endearment, A Ghrá, because that meant she loved me. I was expecting her to say that I was "lucky to be getting to hell out of the oul kip" and would I hurry up and have "a bit of toast and a sup of tea" that would stand to me on my journey. She had said that often in the days before. I felt an ache on the back of my neck when we exchanged sideways glances.

I had packed the night before, putting the strong, laced shoes for working around the house at the bottom of the suitcase, where the gray cardboard was turning yellow. The skirts, blouses and underwear, I placed on top. As she helped me tie the suitcase on the carrier of the bike, Mam kept praying out loud. With each pull and knot of the twine, she'd say, "May the Lord and His blessed mother watch over us."

"Will you give over? Sure isn't she a big girl now going off to work," Dad said as he wheeled his own bike out of the stable, where he kept the straw for the cattle.

"Godspeed you, A Ghrá, and indeed, 'tis a sad day you have to leave the kip so young," Mam said reaching out to hug me. I pulled away from her, because now I was a big girl going off to work. But the bike felt heavy as I wheeled it away from the door.

When I turned to wave, she was looking at the flagstones outside the half door where the chickens were pecking at leftover crumbs from the day before. She looked up, waved back and said again, "Godspeed you, A Ghrá."

Dad and I couldn't think of anything to say to each other as we cycled along the Knock road. I fixed my eyes on the roadside and put the thoughts that made me feel I was being given away out of my mind. The short bristles of grass were silvery white with frost. The low bushes hung with spider webs, glistening as they spread from one branch to another, forming shapes that looked like tiny fishing nets. Somehow it felt right to peddle slowly, but I thought that the only time I'd ever seen people cycle with such heavy feet was when they were following a hearse. Still, neither of us wanted to quicken the pace, and I wished we could think of something to say.

We walked down the steep Cnoc a Bhainne hill, because Dad said we should take our time. "We can go easy. There's no rush so there isn't."

I was glad to hear him speak but couldn't think of how to respond. There was tightness in my chest that kept me from thinking. I noticed icicles on the tree behind Kneafseys' wall, tiny ones that dripped when the sun shone through them, making blinking stars between the branches. Then my eyes got blurry, and I couldn't see the road. I got off the bike and started to fix the suitcase.

"Is it the oul suitcase that's givin' you trouble?"

"Oh, I was just fixin' it so it wouldn't fall off," I said, without looking at him. I remembered that, as a small child, I'd rush to open this old valise, rummaging through his clothes until I had found the bag of sweets. Seasonal work in England would take him away from us for several months at a time. That always caused Mam to say, "Damn and blast the poverty anyhow." Sometimes she'd say she should have gone off to America. At other times, she'd wish she had joined the nuns. I thought of asking Dad if he remembered the sweets in his bag, but I just kept foostering with the twine, undoing it and retying it.

Dad put his bike on the side of the road and undid the twine.

He took the suitcase off, looked at it as if it had committed some sort of crime, put it back again, looked at it accusingly once more and retied it.

"Soon you'll have your own money and you can buy a nice bag with the pound-a-week wages you'll be earning," Dad said.

When we got on the bikes again, I could hear the ice crackling under the wheels as we slowly cycled over frozen puddles. Looking around the bend, I saw we were nearing Knock. I could see the Flynn house in the distance, the smoke from its tall chimney twirling against the black clouds that were gathering above it. Suddenly, I wanted rain—pelting lashing rain that drenched us to the skin. And it came, as it did almost every day, regardless of the season. When the first drops fell, I thought for a moment that we might turn back.

"We wouldn't want to get the Flynns' floor all wet," I mumbled. "Maybe I could start this job another day?" But my voice must have been too low. Dad didn't hear me.

We put our bikes against the neatly clipped hedge surrounding the Flynn house. Ivy crept down the pebble-washed wall from wooden boxes on the top windowsills. I noticed showy pink geraniums in the lower windows as we went up the steps leading to the grand house. The big green door with its stained-glass border opened, and there, standing in the doorway, was Mrs. Flynn. She wore a tweed skirt, a blue linen blouse, and brown suede shoes. Her dark brown hair was in a bun, and she wore glasses on the tip of her nose. She smiled.

"Welcome, welcome to our house. Put your wet coats on the rack."

Dad must have seen a coat rack in England, because he knew what she meant. We followed her into the parlor then, and she offered us tea. Dad said we wouldn't have any because we were just after having our breakfast. She offered the tea again, this time handing us the cups. I was embarrassed when the cup wouldn't stop shaking in my hand.

Mrs. Flynn looked at me as she talked, but I couldn't hear what she was saying. I felt panic at the thought of being left there with a stranger in a big, big house with a second floor and so many doors leading to different rooms. While Mrs. Flynn explained how she would conduct lessons in school subjects, as well as teaching me to cook and clean, I was picturing myself getting lost in one of these rooms and not being able to find my way back to the main parlor. I was wondering where I would sleep, if I would be able to find the kitchen in the morning, and what sort of breakfast would I be preparing for posh people. Maybe Mag was right after all. I'd make a terrible maid because I never had to do a tap of work at home. Mag and Bridie brought water from the well and carried in the baskets of turf for the fire. I was considered "delicate." I didn't have to do any work around the house. Mam said I was too thin and called me a *síog*—a changeling the fairies would leave behind after taking away a human child. To prove that such a thing could happen, she'd recite famous lines about walking hand in hand with a fairy from Yeats' poem "The Stolen Child":

Come away, O human child!
To the waters and the wild
With a faery, hand in hand,
For the world's more full of weeping than you can understand.

"Let you not be lifting anything heavy," Mam would say. "You're only a delicate síog."

But I didn't feel weak at all. I could run and cycle faster than anyone in the village. I wasn't huffing and puffing like my pal, Marion, when Séamus Forde, the Dancing Master, put us through our paces. And so, Mag and Bridie resented me for being "delicate."

But instead of feeling I was getting away with something, I often felt left out and lonely. I wondered out loud if I'd have to bring water from Flynn's well and asked Mam how far away the well might be from their house.

"Why the divil would you have to bring water from a well in a fine house like that? Sure they'll have water in a tap." But then she looked worried and told me to finish my porridge.

Now, here in the grand house, Mrs. Flynn was saying something about a trial period, and I knew she was waiting for me to speak because there was silence. She looked at me with eyebrows raised. When I didn't say anything, she half-smiled and patted my hand.

"I'll show you around the house," she said as Dad got up to leave. When he put on his coat, I noticed a button was missing and that the cuffs of his sleeves were frayed.

When Mrs. Flynn opened the door for him, I wanted to cry. I concentrated on the flower bed all covered with frost. It seemed to fill up with large beautiful chrysanthemums like the ones outside our own cottage. I thought of my mother clipping a few to put on the table when it was time for Dad to come home from England. Outside Mrs. Flynn's door now, Dad looked at me, then at the door, before he turned to leave.

I stood inside the door with my arms folded and tried to think about nothing. I saw him cycling to the road and then getting off the bike to close the big gate that separated the Flynns' road from the main road. He waved to me, but I did not wave back because my arms stayed folded and wouldn't move.

On wobbly legs I followed Mrs. Flynn back into the kitchen. She told me to take my suitcase and she'd show me where I was going to sleep. She led the way upstairs to a lovely room that reminded me of rooms I'd seen in picture books that my friend Marion got from her Aunt Delia in America. There were white lace curtains on the window and a pink floral bedspread on the bed. I thought how warm my feet would feel on the sheepskin rug at the foot of the bed when I got up in the morning. The old cardboard suitcase looked shabbier than ever on the white wicker chair near the window with the geraniums on the sill.

Mrs. Flynn looked friendly enough, but with her glasses on the tip of her nose, I felt she might give me the cane if I should make a mistake. I wondered when my lessons on arithmetic and geography would start. Would I have a class with her in the morning after breakfast, or would she give me a few days off to learn about the house first? She spoke in a kind voice as she led me to the kitchen. She offered me a cup of tea again, and I noticed the sugar and milk were in glass-like containers. I wondered if they were crystal but didn't want to ask.

It took a while for her to show me the house with the dining room, the library, and the bedrooms of her older children, now away in boarding school. These rooms all looked spotless, with colorful bedspreads and polished furniture. I wondered why I was there to clean them. Weren't they already clean? Maybe she would change her mind and say she didn't need a maid after all. Then I could just go home again and maybe go to school like Marion Murphy.

The baby started to cry in his crib near their bed, and I hoped I wouldn't have to take care of him, because then I'd miss my baby brother, John. If I thought about John's hair in a yellow curl on the top of his head and how he was already trying to play the tin whistle at only two years of age, I'd resent this new baby. I might get mad and want to spank his bottom and tell him to shut up.

"You won't have to take care of Peadar," Mrs. Flynn said as if reading my thoughts. "You'll have to dust all the rooms tomorrow, though, because the children are coming home on holidays."

All three were away at school, where I knew I would be if we had enough money. Secondary education was not free then. I knew her children were all older than me, and it felt strange that she was talking to me as if I were someone older and wiser than they.

As we were talking in the kitchen, the door swung open and ten-year-old Maeve Flynn ran in, demanding to know why there was a dirty, ugly old suitcase in her room. Mrs. Flynn looked embarrassed and told Maeve to have manners, that Maura, the new maid, would be sharing her room for a few weeks.

"When the others go back, you'll have your room to yourself again. Now shake hands with the new maid and mind your manners, please."

Maeve tried her best to be tolerant of a strange new girl sharing her bed. She went to bed early and pretended to be asleep. She put her doll between the two of us and didn't say a word to me. I stared at the moon through the lace curtains and wished it were Mag on the other side of the doll. At least then we could have a fight, and I could complain that I felt mixed up. I could blame her for everything and kick her out of the bed. It took a long time to go to sleep.

Mrs. Flynn called me in the morning and told me to watch

as she cooked the breakfast. Tomorrow, she'd watch and I would cook, she said.

Without having to tell her, Mrs. Flynn seemed to know that I was worried about getting lost in her grand house. She accompanied me to each room I had to dust, and after the first day, I knew where everything was and how to find the kitchen when it was time for tea. The older Flynn children came home for their school holidays, and although I served them their meals, they more or less ignored me. I was the maid, and it was my place to make the tea, wash dishes, dust the house and, yes, carry water from the well—two fields away from the house.

The weight of two buckets caused me to stop every few yards because my fingers and wrists were hurting. If Mam saw me carrying heavy buckets of water, she would be furious, I knew.

A month later, my trial period was up, and it was time for my parents to decide if I should continue. After eight o'clock Mass, when the breakfast dishes were done, I was free to leave. With the wind on my back and four pounds in my pocket, I flew down the Knock road on my bike, climbing all the hills. I never noticed if the icicles were still there for the sun to play with or if the spider webs stayed on the branches of the bushes that now seemed airborne.

The first question Mam asked when I jumped off my bike outside the half door was, "What way are you, A Ghrá? Is Mrs. Flynn teaching you the sums and school subjects as she said she would?"

I told her that Mrs. Flynn had no time. The baby was crying, and we had to do a lot of cooking for the family. Then she asked if I had to carry water from the well. When I said I did, Mag laughed and said, "See, I told you you'd have to carry water if you were going to be a maid."

I was going to kick her in the shins like I always did, but I remembered I was now fourteen and shouldn't act like a child anymore.

"The divil fire the Flynns, and damn and blast the poverty. You'll clear to hell out of there. You're too delicate for the likes o' that job," Mam said. I didn't feel in any way fragile but was glad to get out of the Flynns' grand house. ᷡ

CHAPTER 5

THE SHOP ASSISTANT

*I*F THERE WERE SUCH A THING as a blue tree, the twigs on its branches would be like the veins that bulged on my mother's chapped hands. I watched as she placed the cheesecloth over the mouth of the milk bucket to strain the cream into the brown crock. As she poured the skim milk into the blue jugs, she talked to me without looking up from her work.

"Let you be on the lookout for a job as a shop assistant. It'll come in handy if you're as lucky as herself in the shop at the square." She was referring to the neighbor who married the man with the shop.

"Wasn't she no better than yourself? A young one from the country who learned the shop trade and married into it? Sure there might be another shop owner, the likes of himself. You could forget about America altogether. On the other hand, if you're not as lucky as herself, you'll have the experience behind you and it'll stand to you beyond."

"What are you on about, Mam?" Although I asked the question, I didn't really want to hear any more about it. I wasn't sure what Mam felt, whether she wanted me to go to America or stay at home and find someone to marry. I couldn't tell if she'd miss me at all if I did go away.

All I knew for sure was that most young people over sixteen were leaving home and looking for work in England or America. It was my turn to go. When she had rinsed out the milk bucket, she nodded her head towards the hearth. Dad was sitting there in a straight-backed wooden chair, his Wellingtons still wet from tramping through the Well Field with the dog when he brought the cows in for milking. He always looked handsome, even though he wore his old tweed cap over his mop of black hair. Dad put a rolled up piece of newspaper into the fire to get a light for his pipe. Mam threw him a domineering look and pointed a finger in his direction.

"Let *you* go," she said, "and see if there's an ounce a truth to the rumor that they need a shop assistant below at the square."

Dad withdrew the flaming paper and lit his pipe, taking short quick puffs. The pipe was sticking out of one side of his mouth. "Aye," he said out of the other side. He put the paper back into the fire for another light and said "Aye" again. He repeated this several times before he was pleased with the results. Then he got up, took a pair of reading glasses from behind the cups and saucers on the top shelf of the dresser, and began to read the *Western People*. He kept his eyes on the newspaper while talking.

"Why can't she stay here at home until it's time for her journey to the Other Side? She'll be gone long enough, sure."

That seemed a clear sign I was to go to America. I went into the bedroom and reached under the bed for my black patent leather dancing shoes with the big buckles. They were shiny, but I began polishing them furiously with the sleeve of my sweater. My heart was pounding loudly. It sounded like a *bodhrán* when it's drumming out the other instruments instead of keeping the beat. I wanted to cry but couldn't. Why didn't they ever ask me what I wanted? If they did, would I know what to say? But that was the problem. It was always assumed I'd leave. Still, I didn't want to think about saying goodbye to my parents, even if they annoyed me. How could I leave Mag, Bridie, P.J., Tommie, and especially the baby, John? And what would I do without my best friend, Marion? I'd have no one to talk to.

Mam raised her voice so I'd hear her from the kitchen. "If you happen to get a job in that shop below, you could keep your eyes open and learn how a young country girl went about landing a man with money."

"I'm going over to Marion's," I shouted, rushing into the kitchen and grabbing my coat from the nail on the back of the door. I didn't want to hear anymore. Still, Mam called after me as I took off up the cobblestone path and out the road, her voice like a banshee's trailing in the wind.

"If you get a job at that shop in the square, let you be paying heed to the way that woman does things. If you have the misfortune to marry a farmer, you'll end up like meself in poverty." Although I didn't see her, I knew Mam threw a sideways accusatory look at Dad and that he took his eyes off the newspaper and stared into the fire.

After returning from the next fair day in Kilkelly, Dad sat beside me at the fire, his pipe in his hand. He took an ounce of plug tobacco from his waistcoat pocket and began to cut it with his penknife. Then he cleared his throat, nodded his head sideways at me and said, "Do you know what I heard today below in Kilkelly?"

"How would I know? I wasn't there," I giggled. I was surprised he had something to say. He didn't talk much except to shout at Mag for wetting the bed.

"Well, I'm after hearing that the boss and his missus in the shop at the square are looking for a helper. I heard that, so I did."

"Well, thanks and glory be God and His blessed mother!" Mam exclaimed in an upbeat voice. "The Lord never closes one door but He opens another."

I knew she was referring to my leaving the maid's job at the Flynns' in Knock.

I packed my new suitcase. I didn't need Dad to cycle with me this time. I was a year older. Besides, I knew the Cawley family in Kilkelly, having been in their shop often. I had visualized myself behind the counter showing someone the new style of wedge-heeled suede shoes, a pleated skirt, a tablecloth, or maybe even filling a pint at the bar.

Nuala and Dermot Cawley smiled when I came in. They had

been chatting with Tom, the blacksmith—the only customer at the bar counter. There was no one in the front section of the shop where shoes and general drapery were sold. I stood there inside the door and put my suitcase on the floor. The owners left their customer sitting by himself and came to greet me.

"You're very welcome," smiled Mrs. Cawley, shaking my hand. The boss, as everyone called her husband, did likewise.

"When the fair day comes around, we'll need an extra pair of hands in this shop and the bar. You'll do a bit of everything, just like ourselves," he said, nodding at his wife. Then he rolled up his sleeves to wash the glasses in the bar. Mrs. Cawley wiped the counter near the blacksmith's glass before offering to show me to my room upstairs.

On the fair day, as I was washing up after breakfast, the boss's head appeared in the crack between the kitchen door and the jamb. The rest of his body was outside in the hall. He nodded backwards in the direction of the shop.

"We need you out here today," he smiled.

The space around the counter was black with smoke from pipes, Sweet Aftons and Woodbines. The combination of smells—cow manure on boots, smoke, and Guinness on draft—made me feel lightheaded. I tried to focus on the clean glasses waiting to be filled. Farmers for miles around crowded the bar. They must have been thirsty after walking their cattle and sheep to the town, showing them off to each other, and praising their soft fleece, good teeth, and full udders.

"Gimme a pint," someone ordered.

When I filled the first glass, with the white froth spilling over the top, I had no idea who had ordered it. I carried it up and down the bar trying to decide who had asked for it first. Hands stretched out all along the bar, and even though I was a bit dizzy from the smell, I felt a sense of power having something in my hand that so many men wanted. Finally, I gave it to the man with bulging red eyes who looked as if he might curse if I didn't. I was delighted with his applause.

"Well now, that's a great head on that pint. Fair play to you! Be God, and you're a fair hand with the glass. You learned how to fill a decent pint, so you did."

Overwhelmed with such lavish praise, I ran up and down, filling pints as quickly as I could. When the boss came on the scene, the man with the bulging eyes said, "Well now, that young wan has the feet with her so she has. She's filling pints as fast and as good as yourself."

A small smile crept over the boss's face, and I could tell he'd always let me help at the bar on fair days after that. When everyone had a drink, they settled in to talk.

"The red heifer is a beauty surely, and she'll bring a decent price so she will."

"Oh, aye, a bloody good price that wan."

"She will, be God, and the black bullock and all."

"He's a bloody fine class of an animal, so he is!"

When a sale was made, nothing was ever signed. The final sale was made with a spit in the hand, a shake and, finally, a click of two glasses.

As usual, all the women sat huddled in "the snug," a small room between the bar and the kitchen. They entered the premises through the side door, because everyone knew that no respectable woman entered a public house through the front door, much less sat on a barstool. Every so often, I'd take a walk to the snug to see if sherry or port wines were needed, but for the most part it was lemonade and cups of tea they asked for. I wanted to spend time there listening to the gossip. I'd hear bits and pieces, and I tried to delay picking up the cups so as to hear more.

"Delia Nolan and Séan Molloy went to the dance together in Coillte Mach, and now they're walking out together."

That was not good news. I was madly jealous of Delia because I fancied Séan myself, but he only noticed girls who were older and wore lipstick.

"That Kate was in the market, so she was. Didn't I see her and a belly in her out to that?" The speaker moved her canvas shopping bag of groceries out of her way and stood up to demonstrate how big Kate was. She joined her two hands in front of her abdomen like an oversized ballet dancer, leaned back and stuck out her belly.

"Well, she landed a rich man anyway, so she did," said another woman while fumbling under her chin to untie the knot of her headscarf. It was wet with the rain, so she held it to the fire, her head cocked over her shoulder so as not to miss anything.

"Now, there is them that's in it, and they should be ashamed of themselves so they should. Ye all know who I'm talkin' about." Everyone nodded in unison.

"Do you think himself knows at all at all?"

"Arah, everyone knows *but* himself. He's an *amadán*, so he is."

"She's in the place below every Friday, with that young stranger from the North Country."

"And what age do you think himself to be?"

"Oh, he's sixty if he's a day, sure."

"I always said he was too old for her. A young girl like that has no business marrying an old man anyway. Money isn't everything, you know."

Listening to them made me think that men with money were all old, and if you married one, you'd have to go looking for a young one to make you happy. Then, women sitting in snugs in Mayo on a fair day would be talking about you. Well, I thought, I won't have to worry about them talking about *me*. My uncle had just sent my ticket for my passage to America. When the postman jumped off his bike outside the door and handed me the envelope with the stars and stripes around the border, I screamed with excitement. Although I knew I'd miss all that was familiar to me, and was frightened at the thought of leaving my family, I anticipated the wonders and adventures waiting for me on the other side of the Atlantic. "Be sure to tell your Uncle Pake that you'll pay him back as soon as you earn the money," Mam warned me.

In the convent, we were told that money was the root of evil. St. Francis gave his inheritance away to the poor. We were being taught to live in that spirit. Mother Mistress also warned us against eating too much. "Keep that spirit of poverty in all your actions," she advised. She knew well that the postulants who worked with the children often shared their cookies or other snacks. As for me, I had daily slices of Sister Malachy's apple pies. After a few lectures on Franciscanism, I decided it was time to follow the rules more carefully.

Sister Malachy looked perplexed as she glanced back and forth from me to the steaming pie on the countertop. It was as if she didn't understand how I could refuse something special she was able to do for me.

"I should stop eating your pies. I'm not a bit like Saint Francis, the way I eat so much."

"Why, Dearie? Why would you want to put any extra penance on yourself? It's enough to give up the world."

I felt a twinge of guilt because of her generosity but knew that I'd feel even worse if I didn't at least attempt to be more of a Franciscan. I also didn't want to have to mention the failure to follow the rules at our "chapter of faults."

Sister Malachy must have figured this out. She looked me in the eye and said, "Once you leave the motherhouse, there will be no chapter of faults meetings. Mother Mistress won't tell you girls this now, while you're in training, but most of the superiors have done away with the chapter on the missions. It's old. I believe they still practice it in Italy, but that's all."

She blinked when she noticed my shocked face. I didn't understand that American convents could make up their own minds about certain rules handed down from Rome.

"But if it makes you feel better not to eat pie…." She waved a hand in the direction of the counter, where a vase of bright yellow daffodils from the garden stood beside the cooling pie. "If you change your mind, it's here for you. Run along now, Dearie. It'll be time for your instructions."

On the way down the hall, I ran into Mariella as she bounded in the door from morning duty at the boys' house.

"I can smell those pies a mile away," she said sniffing the air.

"Imagine if Sister Malachy switched places with Mother Mistress. Wouldn't we have a great novitiate?"

"We'd all be as big as houses," I said.

Mother Mistress was ready to start her instructions. She sat at her desk in the classroom, looking around to make sure we were all there.

"Sisters, what I have to say may seem disturbing," she said, looking from one to the other of us. "Sister Josephine has left us. She went home yesterday. Now, that is all I have to say on the matter. You are not to discuss this amongst yourselves at recreation, on duty, or anywhere else. Remember, Sisters, 'Many are called but few are chosen.' This is what Our Lord said. Sister Josephine wasn't meant for this life."

When I thought about this, I wondered if Mother Mistress had a special gift to know who did and who did not belong in the convent. She must know I did for sure, I thought. But I wished I had spoken to Josephine while she was with us. She stayed to herself at recreation and didn't talk much—even to Mariella, who kept trying to draw her out. I hoped she was happy with her choice to leave, but I wondered if she had made the right decision. Her name reminded me of the other Josephine, Cousin Nuala's neighbor. I knew I didn't want to return to Nuala's house and hear that angry, drunken voice next door. I also didn't want him "tickling" me when his wife was out of sight. I was fed up with the way he'd get too close—grabbing hold of me from behind and holding me tight.

"Come here, you. It's time for a tickle."

It was exciting and scary at the same time. I was almost seventeen and he was old, at least thirty-five—and he was married. One day I reminded him of this. When he didn't stop his tickling, I kicked him in the shins and told him I'd tell Josephine. To my great surprise, he never tried grabbing me again. Still, I wouldn't want to live near him any longer. I was proud to feel called to a higher life. Nothing, no novitiate test, would deter me from moving ahead with my calling.

"There's something else I must remind you about today, Sisters," Mother Mistress went on as she crossed Josephine's name off her list. Her face looked lighter, as if she were relieved to be getting down to ordinary novitiate business. "As I told you before, it's a transgression against the holy vow of poverty to break dishes or anything else here."

I laughed to myself, thinking I should introduce her to Ron, Cousin Nuala's husband. How many dishes did he break when he had too much to drink and his dinner wasn't ready on time?

"I know you don't have vows yet, but you must practice living in the spirit of the vows," she went on. "Breaking a glass, a cup or a plate is a waste, and it doesn't matter if it's an accident. Now, I told you earlier to save pieces of the broken dishes. At the chapter of faults, otherwise known as *culpa*, you will hold the broken dish in your hand while accusing yourself before the community."

There was a group gasp followed by looks of embarrassment. Mother Mistress paused. She looked directly at Mariella and raised her chin a bit higher as she spoke.

"Sister Mariella, I was passing the scullery as you dropped that tray of dishes you took out of the dishwasher." Her eyes traveled around the classroom as if to tell us that she knew all our mishaps and we had better own up to them at the chapter of faults.

"Now, Sisters," she said gathering up her notes to leave, "the main thing is to speak clearly and loud enough to be heard at the chapter of faults. We will have a rehearsal in the refectory at three o'clock."

The bell rang for lunch, and we hurried upstairs. I had no idea how the rehearsal would play out, but it made me nervous. At least Mariella had something to say. I had nothing.

When the time came, I noticed the floor of the long refectory gleamed in the afternoon sun. I wondered if it had always been that shiny or if, when the novices polished each green and white tile on their hands and knees, they took extra care that day so it would look just right for this chapter of faults.

"One thing I forgot to mention before we start," Mother Mistress said, taking hold of the cord that was tied around her waist and proceeding to put it around her neck like a lasso, "I don't want you to be shocked when you see the novices doing *this* with their cords when they accuse themselves of their faults. It's simply a mark of humility. And lastly, don't forget, Sisters, you are to kiss the floor before you rise from your knees."

When some of us looked shocked, she said that no one had ever got sick from kissing the floor and that we should get off our high horses if we were to become true Franciscans. Mia Mary looked particularly pale at the thought of her lips touching the floor where shoes had trod. I didn't feel good about this either but felt it was God's will and that I should "offer it up," as my mother would say when she'd rant and rave about her own fate in life.

"Oh, indeed, the only thing to do is offer it up," Mam would say. "I have to offer ye all up. The six o' ye brought so much misfortune into my life ever since ye set a foot on this earth." So she was offering us up to God. He would take care of and bless us. She would be forgiven for any sins she had ever committed because she had the bad sense to have found my father, married him and brought us into the world. That's what she was saying, I believed.

The tables formed a huge rectangle in the refectory. The Provincial Superior, Mother Roberta, had a table at the top, where there was a statue of the Blessed Virgin over her head. The table where Mother Mistress sat was at the opposite end. Those closest to Mother Provincial's table were senior Sisters. Some walked with the aid of canes and walkers. The younger professed nuns sat at longer tables, usually eight or ten to a table. Following were the novices and, finally, we postulants. The distance between the head table where the Provincial Superior sat and Mother Mistress's table was about fifty yards of shiny green and white tiles. The space directly in front of Mother Roberta was where we would accuse ourselves of our faults. At rehearsal, Mother Mistress sat at Mother Roberta's table, and we lined up in the scullery to wait our turns.

Mariella had a dreadful time trying to kneel, control her skirt so it wouldn't get tangled in her shoes, and balance the broken dishes. She held a chipped glass in the hand holding the skirt while staring down at the handle of a cup and a piece of a saucer resting on half a plate in the other hand. Of course, she dropped a few things and made us giggle.

I was very serious when I knelt with my head bowed. I accused myself of being distracted and "failing in the exact discharge of my duties." That was a favorite with the novices, failing in the exact discharge of duties. Mind you, I wasn't clear what it meant, but it sounded sophisticated. In the case of the novices, I guessed it meant they got fed up with whatever it was they were supposed to do, like sweeping the halls or mopping the floors, so they took a rest or looked out the window from time to time. I really hadn't been any more distracted than usual but thought that if there was such a thing as *never* being distracted I definitely hadn't mastered it yet. Although I believed this culpa might help me gain spiritual awareness, I felt foolish and was annoyed at myself for not being able to say that I didn't disobey any rules at all. If I followed that line of reasoning, I had the feeling it would turn into a lesson on failing to be humble.

Brigid planned not to admit to her nocturnal checker playing, deciding instead to accuse herself of waltzing to Strauss's music when she heard it played on a radio across the hall from the office, where she helped out with the children's record-keeping. This accusation made Mother Mistress jump up and summon everyone together to hear an example of what was *not* to be admitted to at the chapter of faults.

"That, Sisters, is an inappropriate fault." Her face suddenly took on a look of bewilderment. She flipped her veil over her shoulder and walked away.

"Jeese," said Brigid at recreation that evening. "I thought I was doing the right thing."

"It seems as though Mother Roberta likes some faults more than others," Mariella laughed.

But Mother Mistress may have been wiser than we gave her credit for. Either that, or Brigid's gliding around the office nagged at her conscious. Perhaps it may have made her realize the need for girls our age to celebrate our youth and joy of life, even though we were, at the same time, being trained to forget it. Although The Second Vatican Council (Vatican II) had just begun, the old rules still held, and behind her stern demeanor, Mother Mistress might have worried that the unknown future would undo her vigorous training.

At recreation that evening, she unpacked square-dancing records that were locked in an old trunk. Under her directions, we found ourselves skipping around to a dance called the Texas Star. When she asked if anyone knew other group dances that would be appropriate for everyone, I jumped up and raised my hand. I was surprised by my own exuberance and spontaneity. Veils flew, cords swung, beads jangled and sometimes got tangled as forty-four postulants and novices under my direction tried a foot with The Stack of Barley and Shoe the Donkey.

As time went on, a few of my "pupils" became quite proficient. Brigid and Patricia were accomplished enough to join me in the Three Hand Reel, which we performed later in the year at a community gathering on St. Patrick's Day.

That first night of dancing, I told the others how two years before I had been awarded first place in the ladies' Open Reel in Canada. After that, I stopped taking classes at one of the most renowned Irish Dance schools in North America—the McNiff School. Cyril, the director and head teacher, asked why I stopped when I was doing so well. I admitted that I loved Irish dancing so much I was afraid that if I didn't give it up for a year before entering the convent, the loss might be too great and I wouldn't persevere in the religious life.

"You sure didn't forget it even if you did give it up for a year," Brigid said as we gathered up our sewing baskets, boxes of holy cards, dominoes, Scrabble, and other recreation materials.

"I was afraid I'd miss it too much and wanted to see how terrible it was not to dance. I said to Mr. McNiff that if it was too awful not to dance, I wouldn't enter the convent."

"You said that?" Brigid shouted, causing Mother Mistress to stare at us. A quick movement of her hand sent Brigid's box of holy cards flying across the workroom floor.

"I actually said that," I said, helping her pick them up. "I wasn't sure if it was a serious statement then, but it did come out of my mouth. But you know, Brigid, I felt God would take care of my need to dance or somehow take that need away."

"Take it away? That's terrible."

"Well, if I were not convinced of it, I truly believe I would not have been able to follow my call."

"That was fun, Maura. Thanks for the lesson," Louisa said on the way into chapel for night prayers. I smiled back, feeling happier than I had since entering the novitiate. Although dancing in the novitiate was not a frequent occurrence, I cherished the chance when it came about. I cried myself to sleep that night. It was as though someone I knew well, an old friend, had come back from the dead. I felt a huge surge of joy knowing that convent life would not take her away forever. I fell asleep thinking about my dance life as a child and my last dance before leaving Ireland. ⌘

CHAPTER 6

THE LAST NIGHT

"*D*ANCE FOR US TONIGHT, A Ghrá," Mam said. The neighbors would soon be arriving to wish me Godspeed and a safe journey across the wild Atlantic. My dance would welcome them as well as bid them farewell.

While I slipped on my hornpipe shoes with the silver buckles, I noticed that the light flickering in the lamp's globe was casting shadows on a copy of the *Western People* laying open on the kitchen table. The headlines of our local weekly newspaper reported an increase in emigration from Mayo that spring. I looked at a photo of myself with the caption, "Popular Aghamore Girl Sails For America." I was pictured in my Irish dancing costume receiving a pair of dancing shoes that were a going-away present from the dancing master, Séamus Forde. I closed the paper, not wanting to be reminded of the day the photo was taken. I thought I would never wear my dancing costume or shoes again.

"Sure they'll have Irish dancing in New York," Séamus Ford consoled me. But I believed Marion, who said that everyone in America had to dance like Elvis Presley. She assured me there was no such thing as Irish dancing where I was going. Her Aunt Delia said so, and she knew better than Mr. Ford, who had never been to America.

My father picked up the paper while his eyes stared into the fire. He held the pages in both hands for a moment and then placed them back on the table as if his hands were working without his mind. He wore his best suit and his good tweed cap. His pipe, like always, was in his mouth. Although the kitchen was warm, his shoulders hunched together as if he were cold.

"Indeed 'tis a pity the passage had to be planned before your seventeenth birthday. It has me quare in the head so it has," Mam said.

"Well for you that you'll have your birthday in America," Mag said without looking at me.

The thought of having a birthday in America excited me, but I couldn't think of it, dwell on it or enjoy the possibility of gifts, big balloons, and shiny decorations. That's what Marion said her Aunt Delia told her about birthdays in America.

As I sat by the fire, the earthy fragrance and soft crackle of the burning turf warmed me. Suddenly, I felt a profound sadness when I realized that I was leaving everyone and everything familiar. I sniffed the boxty, a mixture of flour and potatoes with butter that Mam had made for the visitors who were coming to say goodbye. It helped put the empty feeling out of my mind. The sizzling sound coming from the skillet sitting atop a three-legged stand above red coals seemed louder than usual. The calendar that hung below the picture of the Sacred Heart showed the month of May. I had crossed out the first three days and written "The Last Day" across May 4, the day I was to sail from the cove of Cork.

"In days gone by," Mam said, "they'd call this night The American Wake, because them that were leaving never returned. Ah, but sure, 'tis different now. You'll be home in a few years, *le cúnamh Dé*." She tore a piece of newspaper, folded it into a taper and got a light from the fire for the double wick lamp on the kitchen table.

The light of the turf fire cast a glow on the hearthstone. I wondered how different the houses in New York would be from ours, with its thatched roof and whitewashed walls. The dash churn, full of cream, waited in the middle of the kitchen floor.

If it weren't for the long pole that extended three feet above and through the lid, a visitor from the city might mistake the churn for an ordinary wooden barrel used for catching rainwater. When the women and girls of the village came in, they would take a turn with the churning. Each would take hold of the dash and pound it up and down, up and down, churning the cream into butter. This turn-taking by visitors to a house would bring good luck to all who lived there. I wondered if that would mean me as well, since I was so soon to leave. I wasn't sure of anything now.

Through the short, lace curtain on the kitchen window, I caught the rising of a full May moon as it climbed above the hill where the fairy bush stood alone. In its light, leaves swirled in a circular dance motion, moving past the Well Field in the direction of the river.

"You'll be lucky to be leaving this place and going off to America to have a grand life for yourself," Mam mused while taking the gramophone from the loft and placing it on the kitchen table. I could tell she was forcing herself to say these words because of the sigh that escaped from her mouth. I took down the gray cardboard box of records and found the seventy-eight of the Gallowglass *Céilí* Band. I wound up the gramophone and put on the record. When the music started, my feet took over and I flew around the kitchen floor with hops, trebles and rocks.

"You'll have to learn Elvis dancing in New York," Mag said, trying to make some joke about our first *feis*, when we danced in competition.

We were on competing teams. Marion and Patsy were on my team, and we, of course, considered ourselves superior dancers to the younger girls on Mag's team, so we didn't practice every day. We didn't need to, we thought. But as soon as Marion reached out the wrong hand in the chain, the adjudicator, sitting at a table a few feet away from the outdoor platform, rang his bell to indicate he had seen enough. He was known locally as Ferret Flately. His decision to cut our dance short did not put me on the best of form for my solo competition to follow shortly after.

"Don't forget to bow to The Ferret before you start," Mam

reminded me as I headed for the stage after changing my shoes. Well, what with loosing a medal to Mag's team and bowing to a judge who gave them the prize, I wasn't at my best. I needed more time to prepare. But ready or not, when Séamus Duffy picked up his fiddle and played eight bars of "The Boys of Blue Hill," I lashed into my hornpipe with a mighty kick, sending my right shoe up over my head. In the fading sunshine, all eyes turned toward the blue and white sky and followed the flying shoe until it landed with a bang in the middle of The Ferret's table, knocking his bell on the grass. With a look of shock in his beady eyes, he picked up the bell and rang it furiously.

"Bad luck. That's all it is. All you did was that one lep," Mam laughed, trying to console me. "The divil fire The Ferret and his flamin' medal. 'Tis only a bit of silver." She had handed me a sixpenny coin with a greyhound on one side and a harp on the other to buy a fat ice cream to help sooth the pain.

Now, on this last night at home, I was too old—almost seventeen—to be soothed by ice cream. Mam was talking again. I was trying to feel brave.

"You might be better off not getting married at all," she said as if she had been speaking in her head before making this final statement aloud. "'Tis a hard life, trying to rear a crowd like this." She circled the kitchen with her head. "Ye're always on the lookout for something ye don't have." She paused and then stared at the fire. "Ah, but 'twill be different beyond, I'm thinking."

For a time then, she looked out the window into space. She continued in a low voice, as if confiding in someone. "If I had me time to do over, I'd join the nuns, so I would. Isn't it a grand life they have—married to the Lord?" With her head cocked to one side, she seemed to be listening to her own silent response.

On this, my last evening home, I wanted Mam to talk to me, fuss with me, and make me feel special. But after her musing, she began bustling around making preparations for the visitors, asking Mag to hand her the jug of milk and matching blue sugar bowl. Mag was quiet and doing as she was asked. She might have been thinking that in a year's time, she'd be going to America as well.

"You sit there be the fire and rest yourself," Mam said to me. "Think of what dance you'll do when the neighbors come."

"I'll do The Blackbird," I said. "It's my favorite."

I wanted to go over the steps but thought I should sit by the fire since Mam had asked me to. It was, after all, my last night. Dad was looking at the coals that were dancing and flickering. Bridie was trying to keep busy. She kept following Mam around the kitchen. Suddenly, she stood still and looked at me.

"Do you think they'll be larks in America?" she asked as I started to practice a step on my lap with my hands, moving one hand in front of the other as if they were feet. We always practiced with our hands at school when the master wasn't looking or when we wanted to prepare for dance class in the evening.

"What are you on about with larks?" Mam said, turning to Bridie.

"Maura is always looking at the lark behind the reek of turf," Bridie said, nodding her head in the direction of the garden, where the mound of turf that we called "the reek" was kept.

I breathed a deep sigh. I loved the lark that flew out of the hawthorn tree every evening after tea. It soared into the sheep-shaped clouds and sang its long, sweet song until it was out of sight.

I wished Bridie would sit next to me. Instead, she followed Mam from the table to the fire to check on the boxty. I kept the music of the dance in my head so I didn't have to think about anything else.

John was playing quietly in the tea chest that Mam had fixed up with cloth around the rim to keep his hands from getting cut with splinters. He was bouncing a big yellow ball. I had saved up to buy it for his second birthday. The tea chest was old and crusty with bits of bread in the bottom. I felt sorry for him, cooped up there. Mam insisted it kept him out of harm's way. He threw the ball up in the air and caught it. Whenever it came out of the tea chest, Bridie threw it back to him.

P.J. and Tommie were fighting over a pack of cards near the back door. This was a safe place to fight in case they needed to make a quick exit out of Mam's way. If she got angry with them, she might take the rod from the mantelpiece or throw a shoe at one of them. I was afraid that any minute she might launch into her complaints about how hard her life was, rearing six ungrateful offspring. I did not want to hear that sermon on my last night. She might wish again that we were never born. Even though I bruised my toes against the soles of my shoes whenever she made the wish, I said to myself that she didn't *really* mean it. I hoped P.J. and Tommie would stop fighting, in case they'd set her off. But tonight, she just frowned and spoke quietly to the two punching and kicking each other.

"Will ye give over for the love a God and the night that's in it?"

When they quieted down, her face softened even more, and she looked at me.

"Well for you that you're going beyond to America. Maybe you'll go to night school, A Ghrá, and make something of yourself." She reached to touch my hair.

I felt confused. I wanted her to cuddle me, but she hadn't done it since the time of the big snow when I was six years old. I didn't want to cry and risk having the neighbors arrive and think I wasn't brave or that I didn't want to go. So I moved away and looked out the window. My chest felt like it was bound with double knotted twine.

The stars and moon looked back at me. I didn't want to think about going to a strange school at night, but I tried to cheer myself up by thinking how much better it would be than the smoldering fire in the old schoolroom's red brick fireplace that drew steam from my rain-drenched clothes and shoes.

I knew I'd miss sitting on the bench of a long, dark wooden desk next to my pal Patsy Kenny, who every day had an extra apple that she didn't steal from Nearys' orchard.

"Will it soon be lunchtime?" she'd say when our pens met in one of the three inkwells. I'd give her half my ink blotter when it was time to start writing irregular verbs in Irish.

Now, looking out at the night, I noticed a car passing along the road. Its lights cast a glow on the stooks of oats in the front field.

I wondered if it might have been Líam driving by.

I had gone out with Líam in his brother's car the night before. He cried when I said I wouldn't be back for a few years.

"I have to earn the money to come home," I said, "and I have to save to pay back the passage money to my Uncle Pake." I cried when Líam cried and we held each other for a long time. We hadn't been going out for very long, but I knew he liked me a lot. Maybe he even loved me?

"This is your going-away present," he had said, handing me a blue bottle of Evening in Paris wrapped in pretty red paper with little hearts all over it. He wouldn't say where or how he got it, but I'd keep it always. "I wish you weren't leaving me, so we could be together."

I thought I saw him wipe his eyes with his sleeve after he leaned over and our lips met.

If Liam was sad, then why wasn't Mam sad instead of fussing over the neighbors coming?

"Líam cried saying goodbye to me," I blurted out. Mam put her hands on her hips. She thought for a minute before she spoke.

"God help the *crathereen*. He has nothing but a miserable farm like us."

"We promised we'd write to each other. I'll write the first letter on the boat," I said.

"I'll write and tell you about the lark," Bridie chirped.

Voices. It was the neighbors.

"God save all here," someone said hitting the half door with a walking stick. The neighbors turned off their flashlights outside the door. They were here to say goodbye—Mary Murphy and her daughter, my friend Marion, and other neighbors. Even the old people, Anne Burke and Kate Snee, who had been to Grandmother's wake, dragged themselves out to wish me Godspeed.

The women didn't have to be asked to take a turn at the churn. As soon as one pounded a few lashes, the next one was ready to take the dash. They went on with this for I don't know how long. The whole time, they talked about the weather and how the spring was slow in coming this year. Then they started a discussion about the price of eggs and hens. Finally the churning stopped, and everyone settled down for boxty, spread with the freshly made butter.

"Take some you, A Grá, so you'll be lucky in your new life," Mam said.

I wasn't hungry, but no one seemed to notice. I had the feeling they didn't even know I was there the way their eyes kept avoiding me. Finally, Mary Murphy spoke.

"You'll be lucky beyond, I'm thinking. Some nice Yank will lift you off your feet. Don't forget to come back and visit us."

There was silence for a long time before Mam cleared her throat and announced that someone should sing a song. Someone did, though I don't remember who sang or what the song was. When the song was finished, it was time for my dance. When "Miss McLeod's Reel" started, I rose to my toes and flew around the kitchen, leaping between Kate Snee's and Delia Kenny's chairs, around Mam's stool and back again to the middle of the floor. It was as if the music stole my mind and I didn't see or feel the presence of anyone there. When the applause finally died, Marion put down her cup, gobbled up the last bite of her Kimberly biscuit and awkwardly moved toward me.

"Goodbye so. Don't forget to write," she said, barely brushing my cheek with her lips. Then she was gone—out the door as fast as a hare running from a dog. I had hoped she would stay a while after the others. I needed her to keep me company because I wasn't tired and didn't want to sleep on this, my last night.

"She'll miss you," her mother said looking into the fire. In a daze, I said goodbye to the others as each in turn pressed a few coins or notes into my hand before they left. Some of the older people kissed my cheek, saying, "*Slán agus beannacht, a stór*" Others shook my hand and said, "Goodbye, Maura. Mind yourself. And God grant you a safe journey."

At six o'clock the following morning, the sun came stealing in through the window as it always did, as if nothing new were going to happen that day. It showed the dust on the chiffonier and made the scrapes on the dark wood look like wounds. It rested its light on my new, red bolero, which looked out of place there on the back of the chair that was pushed under the table with the basket of eggs on top. Marion had said the bolero looked "smashing" over my new, black Terylene pleated skirt, white blouse, and suede wedge-heeled shoes—my going away outfit. I modeled it for her and wished we had a full-length mirror to see just how well I really did look.

"Did you get everything new?" Marion had asked the week before.

I showed her every stitch, including underwear and nylons. She informed me that her Aunt Delia told her that only young women who were fat wore corsets in America and those who did called them girdles, but I wasn't having that.

"But I'd feel funny without it."

"They'll laugh at you because you're thin. I'm telling you, only fat girls wear corsets."

"How do they keep their nylons up without the suspenders?" I asked. She didn't know.

It didn't take long to get dressed because I had done it so many times all night long in my mind. Mam cooked an unusually big breakfast of rashers, eggs, black pudding, and sausage. I couldn't eat anything. I took a few sips of tea, moved away from the table and put on my red bolero. It was time to go.

"Oh, God!" I groaned.

Dad was the only one not in the kitchen. Mam could tell I was looking for him the way my eyes kept moving to their bedroom door.

"*Muise*, A Ghrá, he's in no shape to say goodbye. The poor amadán is crying below in the room. He won't come up to see you off because he's ashamed to let you see him cry."

"What'll I do so?"

"Sure, you'll have to just go. That's the way it is, A Ghrá. He feels awful lonesome."

I hung my head. I knew he'd been sad because he had been moping around the house for weeks. A few times he'd tried to make conversation, asking if I had everything, if there was anything else I needed for the journey. When I'd say I was all set, he'd shake his head from side to side. Then he'd proceed to light his pipe again, even when it was already lit.

"So I'll have to go without saying goodbye to my own father?"

I took a deep breath. "I'll say goodbye to the rest o' ye so."

But I didn't know *how* to say goodbye to my sisters and brothers, although they all got up early and sat near the fire. Mam looked around at everyone. As she bent down and reached for the teapot on the hearth, she said, "Let ye say goodbye to Maura now and wish her Godspeed, and then go on back to bed, for 'tis too early to be up."

She looked out the window, teapot in hand. No one moved except John, who came waddling out of his cradle by the fire. He looked around at all our faces, holding up his bottle for milk. I wanted to pick him up, but something wouldn't let me. I was frozen there in the middle of the floor.

Mag finally broke the silence. "I'll write to you and tell you who won the Mayo championship next month."

"Oh, do. Maybe it'll be you if you practice your steps."

"Oh, look who's talking," she said, a reminder of our first feis.

"Mam bought you ice cream that day," Mag laughed.

"But then when we got home, I tried to steal your medal," I admitted.

"That's okay," Mag said, starting to come towards me.

"Sorry I tried to take your medal," I said while reaching to hug her.

As we cried together, Bridie pulled on my sleeve

"I'll watch the lark for you. I'll tell you when the *scaltáns* come out of the eggs."

"Oh, do. I'll be thinking..."

I wished P.J. and Tommie would start arguing—anything to break the tension. Then Mam started to cry. She began to pour tea into my father's mug and then back into the teapot again. She seemed to not know what she was doing.

"'Tis a sad thing indeed, A Ghrá," was all she said, wiping her eyes with the sleeve of her cardigan.

"Don't cry. I'm not afraid, and I'll be back in a few years," I said, but my voice was quivering and it was hard to finish the sentence. I touched my new handbag and felt the coolness of the shiny plastic against my fingers. Then I tried again.

"I'm not afraid, and I'll send everyone a pres—"

Suddenly, Mam moved to the door as if she were the one leaving. Mag took a few steps after her, and then Bridie followed. Mam lifted the latch of the half door, and I stepped on to the cobblestone street. Tom Nixon, our neighbor who was the hackney driver, came into the house, took my bag and put it into the car. Then he stood by the open door, shifting from one foot to the other.

Mam reached to hug me. I felt the brush of her kiss on my cheek and the warmth of her plumpness against my new clothes. When I attempted to return her embrace, she gently pushed me into the car. Then she took a bottle of Knock shrine holy water from the pocket of her cardigan and sprinkled me.

"May you have good luck, A Ghrá. May the Lord grant you a safe journey. In the name of the Father, the Son, and the Holy Ghost!"

I felt empty, disconnected, as though I was going through motions without feeling them. I reminded myself that many others were emigrating. Theresa, a neighboring girl, was leaving on the same day. As we set off together, we wondered what America would really be like. I said I'd make phone calls to fancy sounding places like Tallahassee when I got a job with the phone company. Theresa said she'd work in an office, because she had taken typing class. We would not be maids, we agreed.

On the train, I dozed off in spite of Theresa's chatter. I dreamed I was in my settle bed in the kitchen, only a few feet from the hearth. Two faded floral bed curtains closed me away from the world, where the moon's light was pushing its way through the window. Finding a slit between the curtains, it cast a glow on the bare, whitewashed wall on the other side of my bed. In the scene that followed, Mam was waving a white handkerchief as she stood by the half door that kept moving backwards. My father, standing behind her, was barely visible because the smoke from his pipe turned into a fog.

At Cobh Harbor in Cork, we boarded the ship for New York. Eating the chocolate helped me keep my eyes off the shoreline. I didn't want to see it grow smaller. Some people were waving white handkerchiefs, and others cried aloud.

I said to Theresa that Marion told me her Aunt Delia said American chocolate bars were as big as cabbage leaves. She said that if everyone in America ate chocolate bars like that, Yanks must be fat people. I tried to laugh, but a noise that sounded like a whimper came from my throat. I threw a small piece of chocolate to one of the seagulls that stayed on deck as the land and the waving handkerchiefs faded out of sight. ᔆ

Visit Home
Summer 1962

THE LADS: "Aren't they grand when they're not fighting." That's what Mam wrote on the back of this photo of P.J. & Tommie.

"GOD BLESS HIM THE MUSIC IS IN HIM": This is what Mam wrote when she sent this photo of John.

NED MIGHT OBLIGE WITH A RIDE: Ned, the donkey, is not at all sure he wants Tommie on his back. John stands guard.

TOMMIE, BRIDIE & JOHN WITH NED: They are off to the bog to fetch the turf to keep the fire burning. This photo was taken in 1972.

OUT FOR A CYCLE: Bridie with her bike on the bóthairín leading up to our old house.

CHAPTER 7

Night Sounds

*S*LEEPING IN THE NOVITIATE DORMITORY was a challenge. Only curtains and four feet of space separated me from the postulant in the next bed. She cried herself to sleep every night for a month until, like Josephine, she too went home.

I listened to the lonesome sound of the foghorn and tried to visualize the Hudson River gleaming under the autumn moon, but the vaults where we had buried the nun a few weeks earlier were what came to me. In my mind's eye, I watched the procession that formed a semicircle around that burial chamber. The professed nuns lined up from youngest to oldest as they followed behind the novices. With heads high, they chanted the appropriate psalm without looking at their *Liturgy of the Hours*. Some, with heads bowed, looked like the pictures of saints on holy cards. From the serenity on their faces, I thought they surely must have been communicating with God. These, I decided, are the ones I want to be like. But when I dozed off, my subconscious thought differently.

I looked around for the flowery shirtwaist dress I wore on entrance day. When it did not materialize, I remembered that all our worldly clothes had been taken from us and given to the poor. I removed my

*flannel nightdress and pulled on the granny knickers and black cotton
hose that were held up by a garter belt. The blue-checkered slip with a
drawstring around the waist hung loose on my slim body. My fingers
closed the snaps of the long-sleeved black blouse, while the ankle-length
black pleated skirt detached itself from the hanger, flew over my head,
and then draped itself over the slip. Finally, the cape, which was
hanging on the back of the chair in my cell, presented itself in midair.
When this was fastened around my shoulders, I threw open the curtains
that surrounded my bed. It was time to go. The six-inch, silver crucifix,
a sign that I had chosen death to the world, remained on the nightstand.
I did not want to pick it up by its black string and put it around my
neck. It seemed I was ready to leave without it.*

The foghorn interrupted my nocturnal adventure. Listening to
its drone kept me awake and sent me thinking about the ship that
brought me to these shores.

When my traveling companion, Theresa, and I entered our third-
class cabin, two English girls were already settled in. They looked at
Theresa and me as if we were the plague.

"Oh blyme, two Irish bogtrotters. Fuck off, you two. This
cabin's taken," the big blond one said. She was lying on the lower
bunk to the right of the cabin door, wearing only knickers and a
bra. Her hair was in a French twist. Her lipstick was a bright shade
of red. I frantically turned to run out. Theresa followed. Out in the
corridor, I glanced to see if my ticket matched the number on the
door. It did, so back in we went. I held my ticket in front of me like
a criminal holding a prison number. The other cabin occupant,
less gaudy than the blond, said, "Bloody 'ell!" Her long, straight
black hair fell loose over her shoulders. She sat on the lower bunk
on the opposite side of the cabin with her glasses on the tip of her
long nose and her blue high-heeled shoes dangling off her large
feet. She stopped putting on eye shadow and stared at us.

"Dunno, Liz," she said looking at the blond. "There's four
bleedin' bunks in 'ere."

Liz jumped up and snatched the cabin ticket out of my hand.

She squinted at it and then turned it over and over as if she couldn't believe her eyes.

"Give that ticket back, you rude slob," I managed to say. I was not feeling as brave as I pretended to be. Liz stuck out her tongue at me.

"That's childish," said Theresa. "If you can't be civil, we'll go and tell the captain."

"I'll have to move over to your side, Liz," said the dark-haired one as she gathered up her underwear and nylons that were scattered around on the top bunk.

Liz angrily pelted a garish-looking pair of gold-colored slingback shoes into the drawer under her bunk. Then she heaved a pile of clothes that were strewn on the top bunk onto the shoes in the drawer. Next, she threw on her dressing gown, and without bothering to tie it closed, she left the cabin. When she returned, she had a long piece of rope.

"Jaysus," said Theresa. "What the hell do you think your doin' with the rope?"

"You speak when you're spoken to," Liz snapped. "This side ova 'ere is our side—the English side. Don't cross that bleedin' rope," she demanded while setting the thick twine down on the middle of the narrow cabin floor. Then she took duct tape out of her robe pocket, secured her line of division between us and stated firmly, "You two stay on your own side."

Theresa and I burst into a fit of laughter when we saw that we'd have to walk sideways if we didn't want to cross the rope and land in England. Theresa started shuffling sideways, pretending to dance.

"Hop one, two, three, four, five, six, seven," I sang, lilting to "Miss McLeod's Reel." The two stared at us with incredulous expressions.

"Let's get out of here and go up on deck," I said after we put our cardboard suitcases at the head of the bunks on our side. We wandered around trying to avoid watching people who were seasick from the stuff they drank before getting on board.

That night and every night during the seven-day crossing, I awoke to panting and moaning. The first night, too scared to move, I lay frozen, wondering if one of the two women on the English side was being attacked. But there were giggles, too. And if Liz was being hurt, why would she say "yes, yes" with such excitement?

The noise Liz's visiting sailor was making I'd heard before. My bed, when I was nine, was set up alongside the window where the rose bush tried to look in. My parents' bed was against the wall on the other side of the small, whitewashed room. It was winter, so topcoats were spread over the blankets for added warmth.

"Leave me alone, you oul amadán. Don't we have enough mouths to feed as it is?" Mam said. "By rights, we shouldn't be in this predicament at all," she added with a giggle.

Dad said nothing. He groaned like the sailor.

I sprang up from my small bed, unable to bear my father's grunts and moans. The moon, big and round, shone through the two small lace curtains with the red ribbon that Mam had tied in a bow between them to welcome Dad home from England.

The shadow on the wall was a moving hill. It rose up and down, up and down, in rhythm with the moans. I could see the sleeves of the topcoats dipping low and rising again where they hung off the side of the straw mattress. Was he hurting her? Why had she said to leave her alone?

"Leave Mam alone! Leave her alone!" I screamed. Silence. The hill stood still. My mother's muffled laughter both frightened and confused me. She said nothing to assure me, but I knew there was something between them that should not be shared with me.

I lay back down, confused, and stayed awake long after the hill flattened and the snoring rose like thunder.

In the morning, my father came to kiss me good morning, as he always did. I noticed him differently that day as he got out of bed. I turned my face to the wall when he came for his morning kiss.

"Oh, give Daddy a kiss like always. Come on," he pleaded, his beard rough against my cheek.

"No! Go away!" I shouted, covering my head with my pink, striped blanket.

He slunk away, back to his side of the room, and put on his

trousers. I knew he was finished putting them on when I heard him take his belt from the back of the chair. I recognized the clang of the buckle because it made the same sound when he was angry and took it off to wallop Mag for wetting the bed or P.J. and Tommie for fighting or going fishing on school days. Then, like on the ocean liner, there was no place to go to get away from the discomfort I felt.

On the ship, I wished I had a belt to threaten Liz and her sailor and chase them out so that I could go back to sleep. I banged on Theresa's bunk above me with my foot, hoping she'd wake up and think of someplace we could hide. I wanted to get out of that cabin in case the sailor tumbled out of Liz's berth. If he did, he might roll across the rope and end up on the floor right beside me.

I tried to lie as still as a corpse and hoped they'd start snoring soon. I made Theresa switch bunks with me after the second night.

Since the sexual encounters accompanied by loud moans kept me awake night after night, it must have had a huge effect on me. I can't remember anything else about my seven days at sea. My brother John later reminded me that I sent home a postcard of the ship. On the back I had written, "This is the ship that took me three thousand miles away from home."

Thinking about this in the novitiate kept me awake. I watched the thin moon hover as the morning's light broke through the gauze curtains of the dormitory window. Although there was no clock to tell me the time, I knew it must be almost five in the morning, the time when Sister Giancarla, the assistant novice mistress, would wake the postulants and novices. I could hear the rustle of her beads as she walked through the dormitory with a quick confident step, bell in hand. I prepared my ears and felt sorry for those who were summoned from a sound sleep by the loud peal of that brass bell.

With her white towel around her head and her black bathrobe zipped up, Claudia stepped hurriedly into her slippers to rush back to the dorm. She was always first into the bathroom, moving with a fierce briskness that made me nervous just to look at her. She would be the first one dressed and in line for chapel, as always. I wondered what she was rushing for. It wasn't as if she was going to win a prize or something. I wanted to ask her why she always needed to be first, but I never did.

Although tired on that morning, I knew I would not be last. Brigid, who was not a morning person, would have stayed in a state of slumber until the toll of angelus bell at noon if she had her way. She was always last. On my way out of the shower room, I noticed the dragging slippers emerging from behind her curtain. It looked like she would be late to chapel, but, as usual, she made it at the very last moment.

After morning prayers, Mass and breakfast one day, Mother Mistress told us about the two people who founded our particular Franciscan order. She told us that a hundred years ago, a young French widow, Laura Leroux, wife of the Duke of Bauffremont, was eager to start a convent. She wanted to help the poor, and so she approached an Italian Franciscan priest, Father Gregory, who, according to the wish of the duchess, set up this new convent in Gemona del Friuli on April 21, 1861. The new order flourished, and four years later, the American province was born. The Sisters, new to America, would serve immigrants, orphans, and the poor.

"Just imagine," Mother Mistress said, "what it must have been like for those first Sisters of our community, what it must be like when you first move to a new country. Of course, you postulants rode in cars, planes and boats, so you have no idea about adjusting to a new culture."

I was furious. I raised my hand, wanting to let her know that all I ever rode was an ass and cart and a bike, and that I certainly did have some idea of what it was like to move to a new country, but she ignored my hand. I guessed that she wanted to keep me from feeling special so that I might learn humility. Or perhaps she didn't want to admit she might be rash in assuming that not one of us had some idea of what landing in a new country was like. ᔕ

CHAPTER 8

WELCOME TO AMERICA

*I*T WAS MAY 10, 1958, WHEN I SAW Lady Liberty. We had been seven days at sea, and there was great noise and commotion among the passengers, so I rushed to the top deck for a better view.

"There she is, welcoming us," Theresa said.

"Are you scared?" I asked her.

"Kinda."

"Me, too. But everything will be new. New York, new clothes…"

"New people," Theresa added.

Then panic came over me. Would I recognize Cousin Nuala and Uncle Pake? I hadn't seen my cousin since she went to America eight years earlier. She was married now with three children. When I was born, Nuala was ten, and my mother enlisted her to help take care of me. Nuala always let me know she did not like having to wash my shitty nappies. Now, she would take care of me again. I tried not to think about it. I hoped she had forgotten how she had to fill up the tin tub with rainwater from the barrel outside the cart house, where our donkey's red and blue cart was kept, and how her hands were raw and sore from scrubbing with brown soap on the wooden washboard.

The passport checkpoint took hours. I felt dazed as we were ushered from one queue to another and found it difficult to understand the American twang of the officials checking our papers. I had no real exposure to other accents or cultures except for two English children who visited the village in the summer with their Irish parents.

When we finally filed into the meeting area, I worried I'd not be able to find Uncle Pake and Cousin Nuala in the crowd of waving greeters shouting out names. Theresa saw her aunt right away. Then, with a quick hug, she was gone.

I'm alone in America, I thought as I stood frozen, watching people being hugged and welcomed. I stared at the sea of faces until….

"Grandfather raised from the dead," I whispered. The man I was staring at had the same gray hair and mustache as Grandfather. His shoulders were broad, too, but he wasn't as tall. He wore a navy blue suit with a striped blue tie. He was talking to a girl my age. I waited. He thinks she's me, I thought. The girl shook her head and walked on. He looked around again, searching.

"Uncle Pake!"

His blue eyes sparkled in a smile that was a mixture of mockery and relief.

"Well, you little greenhorn. You can't go running up to strange men in New York. But, yes, it's me."

He gave me a hug, took my bag, and yelled over his shoulder, "She's here!"

Nuala, who had been watching the new arrivals from the other side, came rushing over with her husband, Ron. Nuala had the same round face with rosy cheeks that I remembered. She wore a cotton print dress and sandals without stockings. Ron, a dark-haired. stocky man with brown eyes, said, "Is this the greenhorn?" They all hugged me and said, "You're welcome to America. Let's go home."

Home? It was only seven days ago since Mam sprinkled me with holy water and waved her white handkerchief in front of the door to the cottage which, until now, was home.

"It's hot," I said, wiping sweat from my forehead.

"It's only May. This is nothing," Nuala said as she grabbed my bag. Then Ron took it from her.

"I didn't have much clothing I wanted to bring," I said after noticing how light my bag seemed to be in Ron's big hands. "I'll get a job and buy more clothes tomorrow," I said. They all laughed, and Uncle Pake called me a greenhorn again.

"Don't listen to Pop," Nuala said, hugging my shoulders. "He's only kidding."

"Pop?" I asked.

"That's what they call their fathers in America—Pop." Then she added, "I remember when I first came. They called me a greenhorn as well."

Their speech sounded a little strange—part Irish and part Yank.

As we drove to their home in Long Island, I stared out the window, marveling at the size of the cars. They looked awkward, bigger even than the gypsy caravans that needed two horses to pull them along narrow Mayo roads. They seemed too close together and moved slowly, as if there was a funeral or something.

"God damn traffic," Ron mumbled.

In comparison to the small cottages of Mayo, the houses looked austere. They had no fields in front or in back. I wondered where children played. I noticed the houses had chimneys, but no smoke came from them.

"They don't need fires in Long Island in May," Nuala said when she saw I was straining my neck to look at chimneys.

Finally, we stopped in front of a gray house that was so close to its neighbors on both sides that all three houses were connected.

"Here we are," Nuala said as we got out of the car. My new family took me upstairs to the second floor of their house. Nuala showed me my room, next to Uncle Pake's. Nuala's and Ron's bedroom was downstairs off the living room. A kitchen and bathroom were also on the first floor. The house reminded me of the Flynns' house, but it was Nuala's job to clean this one. They suggested that I'd get a job with the phone company and pay twenty dollars a month for my room and board.

"I want to join a dance class," I said. "That way, I'll keep up my dancing skills."

"You'll need money to pay for the class. First things first," said Uncle Pake. ☙

CHAPTER 9

FIRST JOB IN AMERICA

OUSIN NUALA SET HER MOUTH in a straight line and made wrinkles between her eyes as she turned her head to one side and looked at me.

"You'll *know* the answers. Like I said, they'll probably just give you a written and oral test of some sort to make sure you can read and write. You'll be fine, so cut out the worrying."

The next morning, she took me to the New York Telephone Company's main office on Lexington Avenue. It was my first time in the subway. When we got on the C train at Grand Avenue in Elmhurst, I felt people were watching me. I suspected it must have been because I was the new person on the train that day. I asked Nuala if she knew people on the train and if they were all her neighbors. She looked at me with her mouth open. Then she laughed. "I remember when I first came here, too," she said. "You have to stop talking like a greenhorn. No one knows anyone on the subway. You gotta remember the city is different from the country. New York is a big city. It's a lot different from Aghamore. Once you learn how to hold on and not stagger and fall when the train jolts, no one will take any notice of you."

I held on to the pole in the center of the car, and, indeed, people stopped looking at me. I felt self-conscious just the same, so I tried to focus on the advertisements around the car. It was then that I realized I knew nothing about American money. Some ads showed prices, but I didn't know what they meant.

"I don't know the money yet," I said in a panic.

"Nothing to it," Nuala said. "I'll show you later."

We changed at Jackson Heights to the E train and took that to Lexington and 59th Street. From there, we walked to the telephone company office.

I was a wreck with worry, but it was just as Nuala had said. A woman introduced herself as Miss Waters, the chief operator. She asked me my name, how long I was in the U.S., if I liked New York, and other simple questions. I had the feeling that how I spoke was more important to her than what I actually said. She listened carefully, cocking her head to one side and asking me to repeat the word "Elmhurst." I was nervous she was going to say my accent was too strong.

"You seem like a nice young lady," she said. Then she left.

A clerk handed me a form and asked me to fill it out. It asked for basic information: my address, age and date of birth. All was well until I came to "Name of High School." How was I to answer? I sat biting the pencil and wondered if I should put down the word "none." I went over it in my mind. Name of high school: none. Would they think I was an honest worker and a good person for telling the truth? Would they think I didn't know anything? What if they thought I went to high school and didn't pass? A woman came to the desk and asked if I was almost finished filling out the form. "Almost," I said. Quickly, I filled in the space with "Dubh Gara," the name of my two-room elementary schoolhouse, where the schoolmaster loved to use his cane. If the phone company doesn't know it's not a high school, it's not my fault, I thought.

I wondered if they'd ask what subjects I learned in this school that they never heard of. I wondered if they would ask what the name Dubh Gara meant and what they would ask when I told them: "And what did you learn in the Black Garden?"

But when Miss Waters returned, she said, "Young lady, you can start your new job as a long-distance operator at the Eldorado Five Office as soon as you pass the medical exam we scheduled for you."

Nuala took me to Schrafts for ice cream. "It's time to celebrate," she said. When she introduced me to an acquaintance of hers who worked there, Nuala announced, "This greenhorn just got a job at the telephone company."

When I got word that I had passed the physical and it was time to start training, I realized I had forgotten the subway route. So Uncle Pake took it upon himself to take me to work on the first day. He said I should pay attention so I'd know how to get there myself the following day. I followed him down the subway steps at Elmhurst Avenue. He didn't wait for me to catch up, didn't turn around to make sure I was following. He kept hurrying as if I weren't with him at all. I remembered to grab hold of the pole so I wouldn't fall. I turned to sneak a look at a black man who smiled at me. Then I felt Uncle Pake punch me hard on the arm. "You're not at home now," he said out of the side of his mouth. He shook my arm then and warned me not to look at people, to keep my bag under my arm and, whatever else I do, not to engage anyone in conversation—especially the coloreds.

"What's the coloreds?"

The doors were closing and the train was starting to move, making its rumbling noise. He leaned in towards me and spat the word "coloreds" again out of the side of his mouth, nodding toward the black man.

"I was just lookin' at him. He looks so different! Oh, look, there's more! Look at the woman and the two lovely little dark girls."

"Will you cut it out? You're not back in Aghamore. This here is different." He was whispering in my ear and looked around like a fox about to attack a henhouse.

"You never saw anyone that color before, but you can't keep gawking at them like a greenhorn."

"I'm tired of everyone calling me a greenhorn!"

"Mind yourself now. There. Look over there," he said when the subway door opened.

"That's a Spic asleep on the bench. You have to watch out for that lot as well. Don't be looking at him."

"Well, why are you pointing him out if I'm not supposed to look at him? You *told* me to look at him, you crazy uncle."

"You need to be careful is all I'm saying."

"I don't believe these people would hurt me. Anyway, what does that mean—a Spic?"

He said nothing but nudged me in the arm, putting his finger to his lips. He looked straight ahead of him into space.

"I'm able to take care of myself. Stop trying to frighten me," I said when we got off the C train to change to the E at Jackson Heights.

"Well and good. Don't mind me. I've only been here thirty-five years. I learned nothin' in all that time, is it?"

He glared at me, and I felt the fear in his look. He was genuinely afraid of the people he was warning me about. Then, in whispered tones, as we boarded the E, he told me that his nephew, my cousin Pat, was shot in the side of his face as he transported subway tokens from the booths to the central office where he was employed.

"Held up by two colored thugs he was and shot. The bullet is still lodged in the side of his face." Then in an audible voice he said, "Now will you believe me that you have to watch out for them?"

I nodded, but when I saw police with guns, I pointed and put my hand over my mouth. They seemed a lot scarier to me than people with dark skin riding the subway.

"God help you, you greenhorn! You have a lot to learn," Uncle Pake said.

When we got off at 59th Street, I was a wreck, wondering how in the world I'd know and remember everything I was learning. As before, my uncle didn't walk beside me. Instead he ploughed on ahead of me like a dog that wants to lead its walker. ✑

CHAPTER 10

First Friends in America

*T*HE IRISH INSTITUTE ON WEST 48TH STREET advertised a feis to be held on the grounds of Dunwoody Seminary in Yonkers. I had my dance costume from home, so I convinced Cousin Nuala to come with me. I wanted to enter a dance competition and meet other people interested in Irish dancing in New York.

The number of competitors and different dance schools amazed me when I entered the building. I managed to find the entry desk and attempted to sign up for a competition.

"What school?" I was asked.

"Oh, I just came here a month ago. The Ford School in Mayo. I'm not in any New York school yet, but I'll find one. Today!"

The woman smiled, added my name to the list and gave me a number to wear on the front of my dress. Although I kept listening for my number to be called, I missed my turn to dance because I was at the wrong stage. I was used to one platform—the same stage for every competition. But this was big, with several competitions going on concurrently. I couldn't figure out how dancers knew where to queue up.

"The sooner you join a school, the easier it will be for you," someone said in my ear. "You'll know where to go because you just will."

She wore a simple green costume with a Celtic knot. It was the dance dress I liked best out of the scores of costumes there. Her name was Sheila Butler. She told me she belonged to the McNiff School—the one that had been winning most of the first prizes for the last few years. She introduced me to Joan McNiff, who in turn introduced me to her brother Cyril, the director and teacher of the school. The following week, I had the first of many classes at CBS Studios on Broadway at 53rd Street. As a member of the McNiff School, I would be able to wear the costume I admired and wouldn't feel alone as a competitor at the next feis.

When I talked to Cousin Nuala about making new friends, she reminded me that after Mass on Sundays, people mill about and talk. "You might make friends there," she suggested. A few weeks later, while she chatted with someone outside at St. Bartholomew's Church in Elmhurst, a strawberry blond girl named Susan Hogan said, "I'm from Galway City. Just arrived Thursday." A big smile lit up her round, freckled face as she added, "I need someone to go to dances with. Let's meet fellas." She giggled and pushed her strawberry curls behind her ear. Then she said, "You're from the country. I can tell."

How could she tell I was from the country? I hadn't said a word yet.

Back in Ireland, townspeople thought themselves above us country people. We thought they were better than us as well. They went to the cinema and took piano lessons while we dealt with cows, chickens, and pigs. They usually had the opportunity to attend secondary school and always had money.

It must have been my bare hands that gave me away that day. Susan wore a blue dress with a flared skirt, white heels, and gloves—the style of the day. I wore the same style dress in red with beige heels and no gloves. Making myself warmer with gloves in the hot summer made no sense to me. Susan's small blue eyes glanced at my bare hands. A right *Coillte*, I knew she was thinking.

It was a term Townies used for people who lived in the country.

"I can type. Can you?" Susan chirped. This was a leading question. If I could type, it meant I had more than a primary school education.

"No, but I can dance. Can you?"

"Oh, no. I know you mean that didley-didley stuff. Oh, no. I wouldn't be seen dead doing that. Rock-and-roll. Elvis Presley. College fellas. That's what I like. You know what? Come with me to City Center and we'll do real dancing and meet college fellas."

I knew that if we were in Ireland, Susan Hogan would not even be speaking with me, much less asking me to go dancing with her. So this is what happens in America, I thought. Everyone becomes equal.

"You'll have to come to my dance class first," I ventured. "Then I'll think about your rock-and-roll stuff. The McNiff School is the best Irish Dance school in North America! I go to class every Tuesday."

"Oh, that's old-fashioned. The Walls of Limerick, the Four Hand Reel and that stuff, is it?"

"Yes. And step dancing as well." I was beginning to feel agitated. "It's our heritage," I said defensively.

"Well. But we're here now. We need to get with it. You know?"

"Well, there are lots of Yanks learning Irish dancing. If you come to the dance class, you'll see them."

"Yanks? I don't believe it."

"Suit yourself," I said and made to walk towards Nuala.

"Wait," she said. "If I go to the didley-didley class, will you come to City Center?"

We made an agreement. Susan learned the basic Irish dance steps quickly enough, and we practiced along with Vera from Limerick, a woman who had taken dance classes at home. She, along with her sister Helen and brother Mossie, were singers: The Wren Trio. Vera played the harp, and she and Helen sang duets. Mossie was a wiz on the guitar, and they were getting ready for the Ted Mack show when we met.

"You're just a kid," Vera would say to me because I was a year younger than she was. She had a crush on Cyril. I did, too, but we could tell he had no interest in us girls.

We practiced for the Connecticut feis held in a football field in Stamford. Vera, six others and myself were in the High Cauled Cap, an eight-hand dance competition. It was my first New York summer, and I could hardly breathe, much less dance. The wool dresses we wore for the dance didn't go well with the humidity. It would take some getting used to. Regardless, I loved the High Cauled Cap and couldn't wait to get up on that stage and lash into it.

My excitement turned to embarrassment when, during the double quarter chain, after turning right hands with my partner, then giving my left hand to the next dancer and turning again, I lost my footing and fell off the stage. Pretending confidence, I jumped right back, just in time to turn with my own partner. But Greta O' Connell had a miserable look on her face, wondering where I was when it was time to link *her* hand. I could hear Susan laughing on the sidelines. She had that annoying sort of laugh that rose to a higher pitch at the end: he-he-HE. I wanted to give her a swift double kick in the arse.

Coming home on the subway, we decided that Vera and I would stay over with Susan in the apartment she shared with her sister and two brothers in the Bronx. I was distracted, disappointed in myself for having lost my footing. It was my first dancing experience in America, and I messed it up.

"I always won first prize at home," I complained.

"You're good," said Vera. "That's all that counts. There will be other times."

Susan was still laughing about my mishap. "Good thing the stage was low," she joked. I tried to ignore her, but really, she was getting on my nerves. This was supposed to be my time to shine. How could I go to City Center Ballroom and dance with "college fellas" after this?

The train stopped, and Vera and Susan grabbed their dance costumes off the handrail over our heads. The doors opened. It was our stop.

"Oh, no!" I exclaimed. "My costume! My shoe bag!" I tried to get the hanger loose from the handrail, but I was having a difficult time of it.

"Get your bag quick," Vera said as she jumped out of the train. The doors closed. I was inside. They were outside. The train chugged away with me looking helplessly through the glass in the upper part of the door. Susan, roaring with laughter, jumped up and down and covered her mouth in awe as I slapped the glass of that subway door.

"You're too slow," she said hours later when I got another train back. "You're in New York now, not in the bogs of Mayo. He-he-HE!" I didn't argue. I was glad they waited for me there on the platform in the middle of that hot summer's night.

Later that year, we McNiff dancers traveled to Canada to compete in the Toronto feis. I took first place in the Open Reel. After that, Susan stopped making fun of me.

With Brendan Ward's dance band at the helm, City Center Ballroom proved to be easier that I expected. The band played a mixture of ballroom and Céilí. I was able to do both. Although much more glamorous, with mirrors all over the place and flowers in the ladies room, the setting was like the dances back home, where the girls stood around and waited for the boys to ask them to dance. Susan and I were becoming better friends, and we were fussy about "the fellas" we danced with. We'd observe them on the floor and giggle about the ones we wanted to dance the slow dances with. From time to time, we'd say to each other, "time to run." That meant we were going to act as if we wanted to say hello to someone on the other side of the dance floor to avoid being asked to dance by someone approaching us. If one of us didn't make the getaway, that person got asked to dance by the man with the two left feet or the one who had had too many pints before coming to the dance. We had to be quick to move into the crowd, and I learned to escape very well.

One night I crashed into Brian, a good dancer, when trying to run away from a too tipsy guy.

"What's the hurry? Will you dance this one?" Brian said taking my hand and leading me onto the floor. He was tall with dark hair, a ready smile, and sexy blue eyes. He was my dance partner for the rest of the night. We made plans to go dancing again, and, from then on, Susan had to go dancing with her sister.

Brian would take me back to Cousin Nuala's and we'd make out on the front porch. No matter how much we felt like it, we never went "all the way."

"Maybe if we did go all the way," Brian said months later, "you'll forget all about that idea of going into the convent."

When he saw my shocked face, he added, "I'm only joking. I know nice girls want to wait for the BIG Day."

"So do nice fellas," I said, wondering if that were really true.

"Listen, you're too pretty to be going into a convent. And you don't see me going out with other girls. It's you and you only, every weekend. Are you sure that's what you want?"

I was sure, I said. I told him I had been to visit Mag several times since she entered and admired how the postulants and novices looked so holy in the chapel. "I want to help the poor and get an education," I added.

Brian sighed. I knew he was trying to understand. Many were entering religious life, and everyone knew it was an honor to be called.

When the weather was too cold to neck on the porch, we went inside to the kitchen and had tea between kisses. That's when Uncle Pake caught us making out and kicked Brian out.

People didn't often question one's decision to join the nuns or the priesthood, but Susan never let up on my plan to enter the convent.

"Are you crazy? You like fellas. They all want to dance with you. That Brian is a nice fella. Are you sure you know what you're doing?" ᘓ

New York
1960s

WHEN MAG ARRIVED IN AMERICA: We shopped in Gimbels for these dresses. Of course, we thought we looked smashing in them. Mag is on the left.

MAG LOOKED BEAUTIFUL THAT DAY AS A BRIDE OF CHRIST: But Mother Mistress stopped taking bride pictures to send home when it was my turn.

THE NIGHT BEFORE I JOINED THE CONVENT: I wore my favorite flowery dress. I wonder who gave me the corsage.

VISITING DAY: Marie, a friend from the New York Telephone Company, popped in on visiting Sunday.

THE DAY I BECAME A NOVICE, I SMILED: But, really, my neck hurt in the dreadful wimple, called a segolia. I was glad to get rid of it when the community opted for a "modern habit."

LONDON
1966 – 1976

BRIDIE SENT THIS PHOTO OF HER MARRIAGE TO SÉAMUS IN 1966: Some of the pre-Vatican II convent rules were still in place then. I was sad to have missed her wedding.

**AFTER VATICAN II, CONNECTING WITH FAMILY
OVERSEAS BECAME EASIER:** When my brother-in-law,
Séamus, showed me around Trafalgar Square, I wore my
"mod habit" and fed the birds at "tuppence a bag."

CHAPTER 11

Visit Home

*J*HAD SAVED ENOUGH MONEY from my job as a
long-distance telephone operator for a home visit in
June of 1962. I would enter the convent in September
of that year and would not be allowed to visit again for seven
years. I wondered what Mam and Dad thought of my decision. I
imagined Mam would be well pleased. After all, hadn't she often
said, "I wish to God I married the Lord"?

Where are they? I wondered, looking up and down the platform
after I jumped off the train in Ballyhaunis. The station looked
smaller than I remembered, and there was just a handful of people
who were there to meet someone.

Suddenly, I noticed the hackney driver, Jack Costello, waving
at me as he waddled down the platform. Why is he the only one
I recognize here? Where are Mam and Dad? I angrily asked these
questions to the train as it chugged away past the gray stone waiting
room. Jack Costello was soon beside me, extending his chubby
hand with great enthusiasm to welcome me home to Mayo.

"They'll be waiting for you beyond in the house," he said. "The
red calf is sick, and your father had to go for the vet."

Remembering that sick livestock on a small farm is never

taken lightly, my disappointment began to fade. I relaxed as we drove along the Cahir road. The stone walls around Henighans' field where the local boys played football were the same as I remembered. We flew past the hawthorn bushes, their perfumed blooms wafting through the open car window. Though bushes and stones were the same as ever, the houses and gates looked smaller. The Nixon house that always seemed huge in comparison to our thatched cottage was dwarfed behind two tall evergreen trees.

As the car crept up the *bóthairín* leading to our house, I was filled with anticipation. My heart was almost in my mouth. Jack's brother, Eugene, had just gone to America, so Jack kept on showering me with questions. "Is the work good in New York? How is the weather? Isn't it great that Kennedy is the new president?" I said yes to everything. I wanted him to pipe down, stop asking questions. I was busy looking at the wild strawberries growing on the lower part of the hedge and remembering how, as a child, I used to pick and eat them on my way home from school. Although tiny, they were sweet and satisfying. With the car now crawling along the narrow path, I could have reached out my hand and picked those berries.

Mam was in the kitchen. How much older she looked as she stretched out both arms to welcome me. Her short, thick black hair was now gray. She wore it the same style as always, parted on the right and clipped with a hairpin over her left ear. Her skin wasn't soft and smooth anymore. It felt wrinkled and dry against my cheek.

"What way are you, A Ghrá?" she asked.

"I'm fine. You look grand in that blue dress. I'm glad it fits. I wasn't sure, since you wouldn't tell me what size to get you for your birthday."

"Well, I'm glad you picked out the large size. 'Tis comfortable," she said while rubbing her hand down the front of the dress where the little white flowers latched onto brown branches. We stepped a little away from each other to make a path for Dad when he came in from the barn with a stool in one hand and a half-filled bucket of milk in the other. He had his cap on, but I could see by his sideburns how white his hair was. I thought his Wellies looked new as he put the stool and bucket on the floor.

"I stopped the milking when I heard the car," was what he said. "The red calf is sick, and we had to watch him. But for that, we'd have been at the station."

Suddenly, the three of us were in a group hug, and I was shocked by the involuntary sigh that came from my chest when they held me between them together. I felt as if I were taken out of my adult self. I was a small child after Daddy had come home from England. Mam had swept and tidied the house and put fresh roses from the garden on the table to welcome him. My big blue eyes were on his suitcase, wondering when he was going to open it, take out the sweets and hand them round to Mag, Bridie, and me.

When they let go of me, Mam made a big fuss with tea and treacle cake fresh from the oven on the hearth. When she started to pour the tea, Dad picked up the milking stool.

"I won't have any 'til I'm finished milking," he said. My little brother John, then six, stared at me with large, bright eyes. He was dressed in brown corduroy short pants with matching jacket. His blond hair was in a big curl on top of his head. He was clutching a tin whistle behind his back.

"Will you play something for me on that *feadóg*?" I asked him, preparing my ears for a loud blast of shrill squeaks like a cat caught in barbed wire might make. John nodded, put the whistle to his mouth and played perfectly a beautiful air.

"That's 'Fáinne Geal an Laé,'" I said.

"Miss Frayne said the English title is 'The Dawning of the Day,'" John smiled.

"That's right," I said, applauding loudly.

"No more than yourself, the music is in him, so it is," Mam said.

"When I was your age," I said, "Dad used to open a suitcase after he came home from England and hand round sweets." John's eyes lit up even brighter when I added, "Now it's my turn to hand out sweets."

Like the way chickens know to gather round the half door when my mother emerges with the bucket of feed, P.J., aged twelve, and Tommie, ten, appeared in the doorway as I took the box of sweets from my bag. With knee socks peeking over Wellington boots and elastic suspenders holding up their short corduroy trousers, they looked first at the sweets and then at me. When I hugged them, they smelled of fish and the river. From a tin bucket, P.J. produced a trout, holding it up for my inspection. Tommie looked at the gray flags on the floor when I asked him if he had one, too.

"*He* took my fish," he said, elbowing P.J. in the ribs.

"I did not," P.J. smirked. "You took too long, so the fish grabbed my worm instead."

Mam burst out laughing with a loud whistle through her teeth. She shook her head from side to side, put her hands on her hips and looked at the two. "Lord, God, ye two amadáns should wash yer faces," she said. She filled a basin with water from the bucket on the wall outside the door and slapped a bar of brown soap into P.J.'s fist.

"Throw a dash of water on yourself, and scrub them hands— the both o' ye." She looked from one to the other and shook her head again. The laughter had gone from her face, and I wondered if she still beat them when they made her angry.

When P.J. was finished washing, he threw the soap for Tommie to catch. "You missed it, you gobshite," P.J. laughed. Tommie gave him a mighty kick in the arse, and the next minute they were on the floor wrestling each other.

"Do I have to take the stick to ye two?" Mam roared. "Pick up that flaming soap and get stuck in to that water," she shouted at Tommie.

Their bodies had grown in the four years since I had left home, but they both had the same mischievous look in their eyes. They laughed out loud at having upset Mam and belted each other one more time for good measure before Tommie picked up the soap and went to the basin. While this was going on, Dad had gone back to the barn to finish the milking.

Not seeing Bridie there, I suddenly remembered where she was. She had told me in a letter that she had started working for Father C, the parish priest, and that he was a "miserable, rotten, complaining eegit of a man. He spends most of his time at Ballyhaunis golf links, and I always feel bad when a person comes to the door looking for the priest to give the last rites to someone on their last legs." I wanted to run to the priest's house and rescue her.

It was evening when Bridie finally arrived home to greet me. How changed she was! The chubby fourteen-year-old girl with a short bob hairstyle had become a slim, pretty, nineteen-year-old woman with a perm. Her fingers were brown on the insides, and a packet of Sweet Aftons peeked out of her jacket pocket.

"You look smashing," we said, almost at the same time. When we hugged, I could smell the cigarette smoke in her hair and clothes.

"Why are you smoking those horrible cigs?"

"Never mind about that. Why are you running off into the convent?"

Suddenly, I realized that I didn't know my own sister. She had grown up and became a woman while I was gone. I tried to think of a way to answer her question, to assure her that I had made the right choice for me. I couldn't think of how to say it. Finally, after a few minutes of silence and smiling at each other, I said, "Is Father C still a pain in the arse?"

"He is, and worse. He rings a bell when he wants his tea. I'm not staying with him long. I'm going to London soon. But never mind. He had some people round playing cards last night, and one of them, Father Horan, gave me free tickets for the dance in Tooreen tonight. I'm going with Tim Murphy, and he'll be here soon. I better get dressed."

While Bridie changed her clothes, Mam handed me a cup of tea, poured one for herself and announced, "Lord be good to the days gone by."

"What are you on about now, Mam?"

"Bridie going off to Tooreen put me in mind of the time the terrible thing happened in that same dancehall. Lord, God, it was the talk of the country, never mind the county."

"I know. You wouldn't let me go because I was too young."

"Well, thanks be God and his Blessed Mother I didn't let you go. It might have been yourself he went after, the Lord save us."

I laughed remembering the story of a dapper stranger everyone said appeared at a dance there. Father Horan, who gave Bridie the free pass for the dance, had arrived in Tooreen to find a small village with a church, a grocery shop, a few houses, but no village hall. In an effort to bring money to his parish, and maybe to impress the bishop, the then young curate set about planning a ballroom. He went after funds in New York and London and built a romantic-style dance hall.

One night, a stranger came calling. He wore a blue serge suit, and his hair was slicked all the way down to his collar with Brylcreem. When he asked a local girl named Bridget to dance, the other girls, sitting on "the ladies side" of the hall, were jealous. They watched as Bridget stood and waltzed off into his arms. This outsider was good looking and suave, everyone said.

"I thought he was a Yank, visiting from New York," Marion had said.

At the thought of Marion, I blurted out, "Where is Marion now?"

"Where Bridie will soon be—beyond in England, in a heathen country. God help us!"

I didn't want Mam to start complaining about England then because I knew Bridie could hear her from the bedroom, so I turned the topic back to the dance hall.

"Mam, what else do you remember about the stranger's appearance in Tooreen?"

"Do you not remember that the newspapers said that girl, Bridget, had a mental breakdown after her dance with him?"

"I don't remember that," I admitted.

"Well, God bless Father Horan, himself and his money," Mam went on. "When he saw them dancing cheek to cheek, he put the lid on the pile of ten-shilling notes and went out on the dance floor to put a stop to them, so he did."

"Didn't some people tell the newspapers that when Bridget bent down to fasten her shoe she saw something terrible?"

"Aye, she did surely," Mam said nodding her head affirmatively. And I could tell that it was clear that she believed the story that was reported. Singer/songwriter Christy Moore wrote about the event:

> There came a dark stranger, or so I've heard tell,
> who said, "Dance with me Bridget, oh what the hell."
> His eyes were a-burning; her heart was a-smile;
> and all the time Horan stayed counting the pile.
> But when the dark stranger arrived with her coat,
> she looked down and saw the cleft foot of a goat.

Even with this story playing in my head, when Tim Murphy arrived to take Bridie to the dance, I steeled myself trying to smother the jealousy that crept over me. Then I reminded myself that I was destined for a more noble life. I would not just be some man's dance partner, and I would not just be some man's wife. I would be the bride of Christ. Once I determined to feel good about my decision, the jealousy seemed to disappear, and I turned my attention to John again. When I saw how many tunes he knew on the whistle, I boasted about him when Mary Murphy came over to welcome me home.

"Sure you could make a record and listen to him whenever you want in America," she said. "There is a new shop beyond in Kiltimagh that makes the seventy-eights. All he has to do is sit down and play, and they'll put him on a record."

"Well," Mam says. "That's strange, surely. How the divil can they make records in Kiltimagh? It's the like o' that they'd be doing in places like Dublin."

"I don't want to make any records," John said. "I'm not good yet. I need more practice."

"You're great just as you are," I told him. "Get your bike. We'll go to the town and make you famous."

As we cycled along the Cahir road, I looked at the familiar houses and noticed there was no smoke coming from the chimney of the house next door.

"The Durkins moved," said John when he noticed I was staring at the deserted house. I wanted to ask him if he heard that the house was haunted, but I decided I didn't want to scare him. I remembered that the Carney family who were there before the Durkins also moved. "We heard chairs being dragged around the kitchen in the middle of the night," Johnny Carney said.

A bit further along the road, Nelly Tarpey was outside her door waving. I stopped, turned the bike around and went back to her gate when I saw she was making her way down the path to welcome me home.

"Lucky for you that you have the call," she said. "Your Mam is very proud of yourself and Mag. The two of ye are the talk of the village, so ye are."

I smiled and said I would pray for everyone. But, really, I wished they had something else to talk about. What if I changed my mind? Would they think less of me then? But I knew I would go ahead with my decision. If I had the call, I was supposed to follow it.

John was quiet as we cycled on towards Kiltimagh. He peddled away as if he was happy to show me how fast he could go. When we reached the shop, he wasn't in the least flustered about sitting with a microphone. Off he went with airs and dance tunes.

When we got home and took the record out of its sleeve, Mam picked it up, looked at it and turned it over and over in her hands. The wrinkles between her eyebrows deepened when she held it closer to her eyes one more time and said, "How the divil did they do that?"

All eyes were on John as we gathered round the table to listen to the record. No one spoke. It was as if the whistle tunes coming from the gramophone had hypnotized all of us.

"I'm taking it with me to the convent," I said. ❧

CHAPTER 12

THE SCHOOLMASTERS

*W*HEN I PLAYED THE RECORD at recreation in the novitiate, Brigid and Louisa cried along with me. I wouldn't be allowed to see John or visit home again until after Final Vows. It was the rule. The community couldn't invest in airplane tickets for foreign-born Sisters with temporary vows. John's record was "put away." I never saw it again.

As I made my way to my assignment in Sister Malachy's kitchen and the priests' house every morning, it was difficult not to feel envious of the other postulants. With animated chatter, they made their way to the school bus, wrapping themselves in their black woolen shawls on chilly autumn mornings. They were looking forward to being away from Mother Mistress for several hours. They were ready to begin studies at Ladycliff, a college run by our order in Highland Falls, near West Point. Mariella waved her handkerchief with great gusto as they got on the bus.

The day Mother Mistress told us about Ladycliff College, she took me aside.

"You, Sister Maura, since you do not have a high school diploma, will not be going to Ladycliff. You will begin your studies here in the novitiate." Her eyes moved from me to Sister Lucinda, one of two among us postulants who had a college degree. Lucinda, a reserved twenty-one-year-old with high cheek bones, knelt at Mother Mistress's feet to receive her new part-time assignment—me. Her rimless glasses highlighted her bright brown eyes.

"Sister Lucinda, you will tutor your Sister in Christ. Sister Maura needs high school subjects. Why not start with your own major, biology?"

While Mother Mistress spoke, I looked at my sweaty fingerprints on the wooden desktop. I worried about learning this subject called biology, which I had never heard of. The following day, I was the only pupil in the classroom. Lucinda, who had drawn diagrams on the board, was talking with great enthusiasm, but I had no idea if this amoeba she was so excited about was animal or vegetable. She continued with great fervor, as if I understood. I kept blinking my eyes and trying to fathom what she was going on about. I must have looked interested enough to make her believe I was following the lesson, because every time she said "Okay?" I'd nod.

"It moves by making continual shape changes," said Lucinda. My eyes opened wide. What came to mind was the shape-shifting *Púca* that Grandfather said was the herald of winter. On Samhain Eve, when time paused and spirits returned to join the living, he told us, the Púca moved about, changing from goat to horse or any farm animal it chose. So, while Lucinda was describing the amoeba's life in stagnant water, I was back in Aghamore dunking for apples, lighting bonfires, and trying to bite an apple hanging on a string from a rafter in the kitchen ceiling.

Although I had difficulty absorbing the concepts of biology, I managed to memorize enough information to pass the tests.

When Lucinda taught a lesson on the life of the frog, I refused to dissect one. I was thinking about frogs hopping around in the Well Field, when, along with Mag and Bridie, I would leap like a frog on the banks of the Glór River. We'd dare each other to touch the frogs' eggs.

"I'll take your word for it that they're interesting on the inside, but I won't cut them up," I said.

Lucinda didn't know how to deal with me. She was supposed to teach me how to dissect various creatures, and I didn't want any part of it.

"Well," she said, "Mother Mistress must not find out that we didn't complete the course. And, remember, you'll have to take a test at Franciscan High School in Mohegan, and there will be questions on dissection."

"I'll pass. I'll memorize every word."

In lieu of dissection, I studied diagrams of worms and frogs in the textbook.

Next on my list of high school subjects was American history. This class was held in a bigger classroom in the main building where the professed Sisters took courses during the summer. My teacher was Sister Mary Andrew, an elderly nun who walked with a cane and was so bent over that I thought, surely, she must be sick and tired of looking at the ground. Either the teacher's desk was too big for her small frame or the chair was too low. Whichever it was, her bowed, veiled head made me think of a turtle emerging from its shell when she tried to look up and put her elbows on the desk. Her shoulders were hunched up to her ears. Her eyesight was so poor that her glasses were almost touching the pages of the history book she read aloud to me.

As she read about Abraham Lincoln and I followed along, I wondered why I couldn't just read it by myself and let Sister Mary Andrew enjoy her old age. When she'd fall asleep and start to snore, I didn't know if I should wake her or just leave the room so she could sleep in peace. I chose the latter. If she remembered waking up to find her pupil missing, she never mentioned it. I must have found the Civil War interesting because, when she fell asleep in the middle of the fighting, I stayed to finish the chapter on my own.

For two months, I went to this classroom day after day and listened to Sister Mary Andrew's slow drone until she fell asleep. After a while I felt sorry for myself, thinking that I would never be prepared for a college education. I worried that when I finished these lessons, I would not be able to pass the high school equivalency test. But when the day came to take the exam, I remembered what I had memorized and passed both biology and American history. I had no problem with English, but had lots of problems with mathematics, which I had been trying to study on my own. I had to take the test a second time after extra tutoring from Lucinda.

I had little previous knowledge on which to build new math skills, and I attributed this problem, as well as my ability to memorize information and verse, to my two schoolmasters in Mayo.

When I was five, Cousin Nuala took me to the two-room schoolhouse on the carrier of her bike. The high wall around the schoolyard kept out wandering cows and sheep, but the blacksmith's goat was able to get in. When I arrived at the gate on that first wet September morning, the goat raised her head to look at me from a patch of docket leaves that were as high as the four-foot stone wall.

The teacher, whom everyone called "the missus," guided me to my seat at a long desk with three inkwells. Some of the older students were queuing up to put their sods of turf in the basket by the fireplace. I didn't have to bring a sod for the fire because it was my first day of school.

When Cousin Nuala went to her class in the schoolmaster's room, I put my head down on the desk. My objection to being in school grew louder and louder.

"*Ciúnas!*" shouted the missus, putting a finger to her lips. "You'll have to stop that noise now. The master will hear you. He'll be very cross indeed."

Soon, we all heard the master shouting at Nuala. "That cousin of yours is disrupting the entire school. Take her home at once and keep her there until she has sense enough to be let out."

I stopped crying the minute I got outside the door. But within a few weeks, I was jealous of my friend Marion's success with school, so I decided I was tired of helping Mam feed the hens and collect eggs. I announced that I was ready for school again.

"Make sure you're good and flamin' ready this time," said Mam, wagging her finger at me. "I don't want that amadán of a master complaining about you anymore."

I told her I really was ready, that I was only practicing before.

Once more, Nuala took me on the carrier of her bike. I looked at the blackboard and copied words in Irish and English. At lunchtime, I drank milk from the blue Milk of Magnesia bottle that Mam had washed out with well water. I unwrapped the newspaper from my two slices of bread and butter sprinkled with sugar. I knew all the answers, and the missus told me I was a bright child.

One day, not too long after my return to school, we heard the master roaring at someone: "A five-year-old could answer that. Go to the missus and get one of the infants in here." That's what five-year-olds were called—"infants." All eyes were on the blue door between the two classrooms as it creaked open slowly. One of the big girls came in and mumbled something. The missus looked at the two rows of infants. Her eyes rested on me. When she called me with a curled finger, I climbed over the bench and dragged myself to the front of the room, near the fireplace.

"Be a good girl," she said, pointing to my shoelace. "Tie your shoe, and then go in there and see if you can answer a question." She signaled with her thumb over her shoulder, in the direction of the master's room.

I told the missus that I didn't know the answers to any hard questions, that I couldn't even tie my shoelaces yet, for God's sake. The missus asked Patsy Kenny to tie my shoe, and then opened the door and pushed me into the master's room. I stood with my back pressed hard against the door, wishing I could stick to it like the blue paint did. The older boys and girls stared at me.

The master's old brown hat and tweed jacket made him look a *fear bréaga* that you'd see in a potato field to scare the crows. His shoes pounded on the wooden floor as he walked with heavy steps to where a lad was cowering in the back of the room. The lad was wearing short trousers and a gray-striped *gansaí* with holes in the elbows. He was nursing his palms, holding his right hand under his left arm and his left hand under his right.

"Now, you numbskull, here's one of the infants," said the master. "She'll tell you the answer."

I pressed my back harder against the blue door, but the master signaled me with a swipe of the cane. He swung it over his head and pointed to the front of the room. I swallowed and pulled my back away from the door. My feet moved slowly, dragging the laced-up brown boots. My skinny knees were shaking, and I was wishing that my guardian angel or one of the saints or even God himself would come down from Heaven and change me into a bird so that I could fly away.

"Well, now, Miss Mulligan, I see you have stopped your nonsense and come back to school," said the master. "The missus informs me that you're a bright girl. Tell this amadán here how many feet are in a yard."

I looked down at my feet. How many feet in a yard? I thought about the schoolyard. I thought about everyone's feet running out there. The master banged the cane on his desk, knocking the globe of the world to the floor. He shouted the question again. I tried to think. It would take a long time to count everyone's feet outside in the yard. I looked at Cousin Nuala. She was holding her hand up to her cheek. Her thumb and pinkie were hidden. Her eyes were open wide, staring at me.

"Well?" the master roared.

"Three, sir," I whispered indefinitely.

It rained almost every day, and we sat in our wet clothes memorizing verse, rules of Irish grammar, and facts about Irish history. The sod of turf we were expected to bring to school was our admission to the schoolroom. If anyone forgot the "fuel for the fire," the master slapped his own hand first to get the rod ready for action. Then he thundered, "*Sín amach do lámh.*" When the unfortunate pupil obediently stretched a hand out with open palm turned upward, the green sally rod came down hard. The sting lasted all day. In an effort to improve his or her memory, the forgetful one was sent home again to fetch the turf. After this "dose of medicine," that culprit was cured and rarely ever again came to school without a sod of turf.

As I tried to memorize information for the high school equivalency test, I saw myself as a small girl, stepping from one foot to the other, averting my gaze from the cane in the master's hand and trying to recall with quivering voice the poem in Irish by the well-known local poet Antoine O' Raifteiri. The poem was about the coming of spring. I recited the first line: *Anois teacht an E-arraigh, Beidh an lá dul chun sinneadh.* (Now with the coming of spring, the days will be lengthening.) Suddenly my memory froze. My eyes darted from the streaming rain on the windowpane to the dreaded cane as it flew over the master's right shoulder. I was just about to put out my hand for the stinging slap in response to the dreaded command, *"Sin amach do lámh,"* when the cane stopped mid-air. I was rescued by my own voice, which seemed to come from someone else's throat. With a prompt from my pal, Patsy, I remembered the whole poem.

Every girl in the school had to have a turn at "housekeeping." The chores included arriving early every day for a month to light the fire with turf and bits of old newspaper. At noon, the master's lunch had to be prepared. Making his lunch meant putting orange marmalade on two slices of toast. To make the toast, you stuck a fork in a slice of stale bread and held it in front of the fire until it was a deep shade of brown. Sometimes the bread fell off the fork, and if the master wasn't looking, there would be an attempt to hide the bread under the coals. But if the culprit was caught in the act, a scolding for "wasting good stale bread" was to be expected. The master had to have stale bread because he had "a stomach problem." If there was no old bread, the housekeeper walked a half a mile to the shop at eleven in the morning to get it. That usually took an hour out of the school day. Mrs. Costello would look for the oldest loaf on the shelf, wrap it up in newspaper, and write out a bill.

The lunch ritual was always the same. The housekeeper spread a sheet of newspaper out on the master's desk as a tablecloth and then filled the kettle with water that one of the boys had brought from the well at the end of Nearys' field. When the kettle whistled, you poured a small amount into the teapot to scald the pot before adding two teaspoons of tea and filling the pot with boiling water.

"Watch the teapot carefully and don't let it boil. Boiled tea is spoiled tea," the master said.

When you poured the tea and set the cup on the newspaper next to the stale toast, you could then go out in the hallway and eat your own lunch. You couldn't play with the others because you had to be ready to come in, take the master's plate and cup, and wash them in a basin. Lastly, you dried the dishes with newspaper and put them back in the press for the next day.

The housekeeper's chores included cleaning and tidying the master's desk. One day, when it was my turn to be the housekeeper, I wore a new blue taffeta dress I got from Cousin Nuala shortly after she went to America. It was the prettiest dress in the whole school, with ruffles around the sleeves and the bottom. Mag had tried to take it, saying it was too short for my long legs, but I said I always wore blue and it had to be mine. Everyone said how beautiful I looked in it, and Patsy said she was going to wear her dresses shorter from then on. When I was leaning over the fire, pouring boiling water into the teapot, the master came up behind me.

"Your skirt is too short, Miss. Don't wear that again."

"Yes, Sir. I mean, no, Sir."

When I told my mother, she went into a rage.

"The dirty brute. He should mind his own business."

The master was absent frequently, and the substitutes, trainees who took over, believed us when we insisted we were always on page thirty-two (or some other early page) in the arithmetic book. This resulted in our not getting beyond multiplication by two numbers. Whether it was the fact that we weren't learning arithmetic or the blue dress situation, I don't know, but the following year Mam enrolled us in Woodfield National School instead, which was about the same distance from home in the opposite direction. If we traveled by road, it took a bit longer, so we always crossed the fields.

Being the oldest in the family had some advantages. One was that I had a bike. Mag and Bridie, however, had to wade through the long, wet grass every morning. This made them even more jealous of me. Having a bike also put me in a better position as a new girl in the school. The other girls befriended me right away.

Another privilege of having the bike was that the new master sent me on errands to the town. When he saw that my arithmetic skills were weak, this jaunt always took place during arithmetic period. I thought perhaps it was because I was too difficult to teach. Whatever the reason, I was delighted. The pupils were working on fractions and decimals, which I had never heard of because they came somewhere after page thirty-two in the textbook. Going on errands for the new master meant I didn't have to look at an arithmetic book. I was thrilled with my good luck. Mam was furious.

"You're eleven years old. I don't see why the divil he can't send someone else and let you do your sums," Mam said, stamping her foot. She threatened to go to school and tell him off, but I carried on, crying and yelling until she reluctantly agreed to leave the situation alone.

The new master sent me to the butcher shop for fresh lamb or pork chops. My task sometimes included buying bread, butter and other groceries. When the shopping was done, I delivered them to the new master's wife at their house. This took almost two hours out of my school life a couple of times a week.

I got back from shopping one dreary day with black clouds looming. I wasn't looking forward to returning to the dark classroom with its dying fire as the only light, where everyone had to wear heavy sweaters and sometimes coats to stay warm. I crept in the door quietly, so as not to disturb the others at their sums.

I was surprised to find the new master sitting at my desk. He had moved it across the isle, right next to Eileen Mooney's desk in the back of the room. She was the only girl fully developed in our class. We all said she looked like a woman. The new master was scrunched halfway between Eileen's desk and mine. My face got red and I became frightened when I saw him with both hands under her sweater.

"And two-thirds equals what, Eileen?" he said, getting up when he saw me.

Sometimes when I was alone in the classroom with Sister Mary Andrew fast asleep, I'd think about my primary school education and my two schoolmasters. That was all in the past, I told myself, though I didn't know how to keep it there.

CHAPTER 13

MAG

*I*N SISTER MALACHY'S COZY KITCHEN, her Italian friend, Sister Reginalda, was relishing a slice of warm apple pie with coffee. Between mouthfuls, she complained about how exhausted she was with all the extra cooking in the main kitchen. Her additional work was due to all those visiting Sisters who would be back for the Feast of Saint Francis on the following day, October 4. She threw her hands up in the air in frustration.

"He give all his clothes and food away to the poor. Why I have to cook more food when he give it away, Malachy, aye?"

The Feast of Saint Francis was a day to celebrate. Sisters who were away from the motherhouse on missions were returning for spiritual renewal. Bands—those who entered in the same year and were sent off after novitiate training to teach or do child care in New Jersey, Philadelphia or New York—would catch up with each other, sharing stories and bits of gossip about the Mother Superiors at their respective convents.

Cutting off the long, coiling apple skin at the end of her knife and then glancing at the two pies cooling on the counter top, Sister Malachy laughed at her friend's question.

"You'll just have to offer it up, Reggie," she said.

I wished I were as comfortable with Mag as these two friends were with each other. I wondered where and when I would see Mag that day. Later, as I waited to file into the refectory for dinner with the other postulants, I thought how I always felt superior to Mag, but now, I was two years behind her in seniority. My mind then became blank. I did not want to admit that I was jealous of Mag. In two years, I'd take my first vows. Then we'd be equal. That's when my mother would invite her best friend, Mary Murphy, in for a cup of tea to celebrate her two oldest children.

I could imagine what she'd say. "Well, isn't it well for them? They won't have a care in the world but to say their prayers. Isn't it many a time I wished I'd gone that road myself." Then she'd think to herself and maybe regret how often she'd said that none of her offspring would ever amount to anything. She'd look at photos of Mag and me in our Irish dancing costumes, and then in our religious habits, and show them off to Mary Murphy, as if she hadn't lived next door to us her whole life.

When she focused on my picture, she'd take down my doll, Elizabeth, from its place of honor on top of the dresser in the kitchen, open the box she was in, and roll down the little blanket that she herself made for me out of an old flannel shirt belonging to my father. She'd look lovingly at the old doll and say, "May God direct you, A Ghrá."

Waiting in the convent corridor for the dinner bell to ring, I could hear the chanting grow stronger as the visiting nuns approached. The procession, a river of black and gray, poured out of the chapel and down the hall. As they streamed into the refectory, their voices, like the droning of bees, rose and fell with the inflections of the Latin prayer: *Gloria Patri, et Filio, et Spiritui Sancto. Sicut erat in principio et nunc et semper. Et in saecula saeculorum. Amen.*

The older voices, deep and melodic, harmonized with the younger ones, high pitched and airy like flutes. Suddenly, clearly above the others, somewhere in the long line of bowed veiled heads, Mag's voice rang out. As the human train of charcoal gray neared the refectory, there was Mag—the very one who arrived in my cradle when I was fifteen months old. The one who made me cry because she got all the attention when the neighbors came to welcome her to the world, placing coins and notes in her tiny hand. There she was in full black veil and dark gray habit—the very same sister I used to kick out of the bed when she wet the sheets. The same sister who followed me to America.

I remembered how upset I was when she announced she had met the Franciscans at a vocation rally and was leaving the world to join them.

"You're only in America one month," I told her. "How can you know it's the right life for you? Maybe we could do things together, now that we're grown up. I mean, you could come to dances and join the McNiff School of Dancing with me. Now that we're older, it'll be nice to be friends."

But Mag's eyes had a look of determination.

"My mind is made up. We'll have visiting day once a month the first year. It'll be nice. You can come up to Peekskill on the train."

"It was a mistake for you to work in that rectory. I should have tried to get you a job at the telephone company. Oh, Mag, don't go unless you're very sure."

But she was sure and she went.

During my monthly visits with her throughout her postulant year, I decided she had grown so very peaceful that God must have truly called her. On that day, waiting to see her in that long line of nuns, the desire to feel she was someone who belonged to me was overpowering. I felt guilt for having been a selfish older sister. I wished I felt more serene and sure of myself, of my place in the world.

As the younger nuns approached the refectory, I watched Mag in the line, detached, aloof. She filed past me without looking up. My heart sank. Other nuns smiled very naturally at postulants they had taught in school. I wished Mag was not quite so perfect. When the chanting stopped, we postulants followed the professed nuns and took our places at the end of the refectory. Mother Roberta rang the bell for recreation. That meant we had permission to talk during the meal. I wished the feast day also allowed for mingling among the other tables, but I knew I'd have to wait until visiting hour was set to see Mag in Sacred Heart Hall.

When I strained my neck, I could see where my sister was sitting along with those who had joined the order the same year she did. I thought she wasn't touching her food but tried not to stare.

Sacred Heart Hall looked even larger than I had remembered it on entrance day. It was here that we all gathered with our families before being admitted to the novitiate. Unlike entrance day, it was now devoid of refreshments and doting parents taking pictures of their girls going off to join the nuns. The tables were bare, the flowers taken away and placed in the chapel.

I sat near one of the six windows, the one closest to the door, so I'd see Mag walking down the hall when she approached. She looked so small and lost in her habit as she floated slowly down the hall with hands under her scapular and eyes downcast. I stared at her, willing her to look up. I took a few hurried steps out into the hall, waved and said, "Hello, Mag. Here I am."

We were about four yards apart now, but she didn't respond, still didn't look up.

"What's wrong with you?" I said with a nervous laugh, becoming annoyed that she continued to look at the floor, practicing "custody of the eyes," as if Mother Superior were still watching her.

"Praised be Jesus Christ!" she said, allowing a faint smile when she reached the door. I didn't want to give such a formal response to my own sister. I reached to hug her instead. Our embrace was strained.

Mother Mistress had often said that physical contact between nuns was to be avoided. Surely Mag didn't think it meant us as well? But Mag took everything that came out of Mother Mistress's mouth as if it were the word of God.

"It's just me, Mag." I took a deep breath, linked her arm and led her to a table.

I tried not to notice that Mag put her hands under her scapular when she sat down because that meant she was being formal and doing what was proper as a religious. I wanted her to be just plain old Mag.

At the Christmas visit of her novice year, I had told her about my decision to enter, too. I expected a positive reaction, but she said that because we had chosen a life of dedication to Christ, we wouldn't be able to see each other any more than if I stayed in the world. I felt as rejected sitting with her in Sacred Heart Hall as I had then. We sat looking at the tabletop. In my mind I saw us as children, fighting for the blue taffeta dress from America.

"I saw it first. I'm the oldest."

"It doesn't fit you. It's too short."

I wanted to tell Mag I didn't know any better then. I wanted to apologize for being the mean older sister, for trying to steal her dancing medal. I wanted to tell her I was sorry about Dad beating her when she and I fought in the hag. He always blamed her, beating her arse with the rod he kept behind the bag of sugar on the mantelpiece.

"It's a rainy day for a visit," I said finally. "Too bad. It would be nice to walk around outside."

Mag nodded her agreement with a sidelong glance to the window. She looked uncomfortable.

"Are you sick, Mag? You look pale."

"I have a problem. I have to go into the hospital for evaluation. I'll be fine with God's help."

I was alarmed but wanted to show her that I could be calm. I knew she'd think it a weakness to doubt God's will. And if it were God's will that she should be sick, then we should have no questions.

"What's wrong with you?" I blurted.

"Oh, it's just a menstrual cycle problem." She waved her hand, dismissing my concern. "It's God's will, I'm sure, and I'll be fine. Are you finding postulant year rewarding?"

"Am I finding postulant year rewarding? We're talking about you—your health!" My voice grew louder. She was sitting up straight now, in perfect control of her posture.

I took a deep breath. "Oh, Mag, before you came in, I was just thinking about when we were children and I'd hit you with my bottle and tried to push you out of the cradle. I didn't know any better."

"Don't think about when we were children. That's all in the past now."

"But your health, Mag. Will you be okay?"

"With God's help, I'll be fine. It's all in *His* hands."

Although I was annoyed that she was acting the perfect nun, I felt sad. On her face I saw the strain of sickness. I wanted to hug her. When she got up and said "Praised be Jesus Christ" as she started to leave, I ran after her, stood in front of her, and tried to hug her again.

"I'll pray for you, Mag. I'll visit you in the hospital every day."

"You know that's not possible. You know that won't be allowed."

She gave the salutation again and walked slowly out the door. I watched her walk down the hall, my face red with a mixture of shame and anger. Was I enraged at her for being sick, or was I angry that we were so distant? Why were we this way? I prayed for trust in God, for Mag to be well again, and for help accepting the sacrifices that were expected of me as a religious.

Postulant year was coming to an end. It was time to focus on becoming a bride of Christ. ᔑᔒ

CHAPTER 14

A Bride's Photo

$\mathcal{B}$RIDIE, MY YOUNGER SISTER, had just got engaged. She wrote to say she would carry red roses and wear a satin dress with Irish-lace brocade when she married Séamus. She would send a photo and hoped there weren't rules to prevent me from viewing it. Séamus, her handsome, soon-to-be husband, would be standing by her side. She had sent an earlier photo shortly after they met. I liked his smile and the way he looked at her with his head inclined in her direction, one arm around her waist. I was glad Bridie had met a nice man. I was also jealous but thought it was one of those trials we were told about in the novitiate. We would have to undergo trials in order to be found worthy of being true brides of Christ.

"Since your parents won't be here for reception, we'll take a picture of you and mail it to Ireland," Mother Mistress said one day when she was in a particularly generous mood. I beamed with delight. I wanted to see what I looked like in a wedding dress. There was no mirror in the novitiate, so a picture would be wonderful. I imagined Mam's face as she showed off my photo to Mary Murphy. She'd hold the picture to one side, look at it, hold it away again, shake her head from side to side and then nod in the direction of the photo.

"Well, thanks and glory be to God! Isn't it a great thing to wear the likes of this wedding dress and not have to feed another mouth nine months later? Isn't life grand when it wants to be?"

But when Mother Mistress saw how happy I was at the prospect of having my photo taken in a wedding dress, her expression changed. She walked away. I told myself the change in her face was just my imagination. She wouldn't have offered to take the photo if she didn't mean it. Wasn't she a holy and sincere nun after all?

As the weeks went by and the reception drew closer, I hoped each day would be the day she'd call me aside, camera in hand. Louisa and Brigid were hoping along with me. They knew how important it was to me. They would have parents and family members come to the ceremony.

"Go ask her. Give her the benefit of the doubt. Maybe she just forgot," Louisa suggested.

"I don't think she forgot," Brigid said. "She's probably on one of her humility kicks. But you should ask her anyway."

I waited until the day before reception to put myself out of my misery.

"Mother Mistress, you said someone would take my photo to send home to Ireland...in my wedding dress?"

"*Your* wedding dress?"

I lowered my head.

"Sorry. I mean *our* wedding dress."

"Yes, Sister, *our* wedding dress. Please remember that you have given up all worldly possessions, that nothing belongs to you personally."

"Yes, Mother."

"Really, Sister, you can't imagine that we have time now for such frivolity. It's so vain! The day before your reception as a bride of Christ, you shouldn't be thinking of yourself in a photo."

"It's just that my parents won't be here for the ceremony. You offered to take the picture a few weeks ago," I stammered on.

"Go to chapel, Sister, and pray for humility. Pray to rid yourself of vanity."

I didn't think of this as a test from God. I could only think of Mother Mistress as a mean woman. Before I went to sleep, I did pray. I asked God not to allow me to hate her. ☙

CHAPTER 15

A BRIDE OF CHRIST

*I*N OUR WHITE WEDDING DRESSES and veils, we twenty-six soon-to-be novices moved slowly down the aisle as the organist played *"Veni Creator Spiritus."* When I joined my hands, placing my fingertips under my chin, I wished I didn't feel so much like a small girl about to receive her first communion. I was, after all, a grown woman on her way to becoming a bride of Christ.

I felt beautiful, even glamorous. I had caught a glimpse of my white pumps with the pointy toes and was mesmerized. I found myself looking for them with each step. I thought of Brian and wondered where he was in the congregation. I knew I must not think of him now, though I did appreciate that he wanted to show his support. I must not look up, lest I become distracted and doubt my decision. To have a vocation and to become a nun was a life superior to that of a wife and mother. Every devout Catholic knew that. Hadn't my mother often said so? "I should have gone off to America! Why the divil didn't I join the nuns?"

I must put these distracting thoughts out of my mind and focus on becoming a bride of Christ, I thought. When I listened to the choir and felt the admiring eyes of the congregation, my face reddened and my heart beat faster. I was doing something worthy of admiration.

We formed a line across the front of the chapel, our faces to the priest. I wished I wasn't wondering if anybody in the congregation thought we looked strange—twenty-six brides and no visible bridegroom. When the priest said, "What do you ask?" we recited a prayer beseeching God to make us worthy to serve Him and be received in the Church as brides of Christ. The priest responded that, by the authority invested in him, we were indeed received. Another hymn was sung, and while the congregation waited, we left the chapel and entered the adjoining parlor to don the habit of The Missionary Sisters of St. Francis.

When I changed from the satin gown to the charcoal gray wool habit, the smell of the wool was fresh and earthy to my senses. I was surprised to find myself looking forward to wearing this tent-like dress with the long, long sleeves that came all the way to my fingertips. Under the stare of Mother Mistress's piercing eyes, I tied the cord around my waist, forming three knots representing the vows of poverty, chastity, and obedience. I looked at my cord and felt a mixture of accomplishment and apprehension.

Sister Giancarla, the nun helping me get dressed, positioned my headpiece—a white linen cowl-like garment called a segolia. It covered my head and folded uncomfortably around my neck. The stiff white band that covered my forehead rested just above my eyebrows and tied behind my head. I took two straight pins and pinned the top of the band to the segolia. When I put my hands to my face, I felt how little of it was left uncovered. When I donned the scapular, a shoulder-width strip of material that fell over the front and back of my body, Sister Giancarla said, "Look how it hides your waist. You won't be tempted to think about your body."

My body? It seemed not to be there at all. I felt hidden the same way I did as a child when I was in a rainstorm and wore a big hooded raincoat that Cousin Nuala sent me from America.

I searched my mind for the sort of joy that, according to St.

Francis, is experienced when you give up everything to follow Christ. My mind was blank. I could feel the sweat on the palms of my cold hands.

Finally, Sister Giancarla pinned the white starched novice veil to the segolia at the top of my head. I exchanged my worldly hose and white pumps for a pair of laced-up black shoes. Now I was ready to re-enter the chapel as a novice.

The organ played *"Pange Lingua."* Because the segolia was tight, I felt a headache coming on that distracted me from the feeling of peace I was expecting to experience. When the pain lessened, the heaviness and unfamiliarity of the new garb made the outside world seem unnecessary. The novice veil blocked all peripheral vision, so my eyes focused on the altar in front of me. This, I thought, is the sensation I'm supposed to feel. But then, I worried about what would happen if one of the pins in my segolia came undone. My feet felt heavy. I told myself that the nuns' shoes made my steps stronger, firmer, as I walked down the aisle.

It was time to deny the world.

We knelt on the hard tiles facing the altar and placed our hands on the floor. We bent forward in prostration, our faces resting on our hands. Mother Superior and Mother Mistress moved backwards, away from each other, unfolding a large, heavy shroud. When they covered us with the pall, the knell of the death bell rang out, signaling death to the world. I could hear sobs and moans behind me. The sign of submission had saddened some of the relatives and friends. If Mam had been in the congregation, I know she'd have been exasperated by this show of grief. I imagined her turning to the mourners with a look of vexation and saying, "Will ye pipe down for the love a God and have a bit a sense? Sure they won't have a care in the world being married to the Lord."

The heavy shroud allowed no light through it. The choir sang *"Dies Irae"* and chanted the *"De Profundis."* I tried to block out the thoughts of death. I didn't really want to be dead yet still physically alive. The concept was too strange to absorb. I concentrated on my hands, the only part of my body that felt awake.

Because the floor was cold, I wanted to pull down the sleeves of the habit to cover my hands. But if I did this, I'd have to lift up. I'll be a distraction, I thought. Better let my hands remain cold. Finally, the choir chanted a psalm that ended in *"Dona Nobis Pacem,"* and the shroud was taken away. When I stood up, I thought I'd feel different, more holy and peaceful maybe, but the light made me dizzy, and I thought I might faint.

Mother Mistress led the way to a reception in the parlor, where we celebrated with coffee and cake as we said goodbye to family and friends. We could not have any visitors for the rest of that year except at Christmas.

"We'll keep in touch," was what Brian, my old boyfriend, said, his face reddening as he bent to kiss my partially covered cheek. I watched him leave, his head down and shoulders hunched. There was a tugging at my heart, but I closed my eyes and prayed the doubts would go away.

Mag was very quiet. She sat with her hands under her scapular and wore a forced smile on her face. My other guest, Cousin Nuala, asked if I wasn't too hot in "the duds." I was sweating buckets, but I didn't want to complain about the weather God had sent on the day of my marriage to Him.

"Oh, I'm fine! I'm used to it already," I said while wiping the sweat that was forming under my eyes, the only part of my body where sweat was visible. Soon the weather would get cooler and I would get used to these strange clothes.

When the families and friends left, it was time to file into the refectory for supper. We had recreation during the meal, which meant we could talk instead of listening to spiritual reading. The segolia made it difficult to open my mouth, so chewing took a lot of effort.

Worse than the physical discomfort of the segolia was something that remained unspoken on everyone's minds. We knew what would happen as soon as the meal was over. Immediately after supper, the workroom with its sewing machines and long tables became the waiting room, and the bead room, where the large rosary beads that hung at our sides were strung together, was turned into a barbershop.

Mariella, who always had trouble keeping the rule of silence, tried to make a joke. "Let's call it the beauty parlor," she said. But this time, no one laughed. We sat at the long tables in silence, reading *The Life of St. Francis*, *The Lives of The Saints* or *The Following of Christ* while waiting our turns.

"How short are you going to cut it?" I asked the novice assigned to the job of chopping off our hair.

Sister Eucharia looked at me with pity. She was young, finishing her novice year and waiting her first assignment. I could tell that cutting hair was not a job she liked. She sighed when she looked at my shoulder-length, auburn waves.

"Well, I'm supposed to shave it, but I won't if you don't want me to. I do have to cut it really short, though. You know that stuff Mother Mistress says about humility and all? I personally think it's a lot of nonsense. But if she checks, well, we'll both be in trouble."

"Okay, I'm ready." I sighed, closing my eyes and feeling sorry for Eucharia instead of myself. While she cut and cut, I tried to bring Christ's life and death to mind, but my thoughts were on my beautiful hair. My eyes were closed, but I felt that my shiny hair was crying to me from the floor. A part of me was dying, and I was responsible for its death. A nauseous feeling took over. I thought of asking Eucharia if she wanted to take a break, get a drink of water from the cooler, just so I wouldn't have to hear the *clip, clip* of the scissors.

When she finished, I didn't want to look at my hair lying there on the floor, so I got up quickly from the hard wooden chair, put on my nightcap and walked through the workroom into the dormitory. As I passed the next novice in line, she greeted me with the customary salutation, "Praised be Jesus Christ."

Without looking at her, I gave my response, "Forever be praised." ∽

CHAPTER 16

The Cloistered Year

WE WERE BECOMING ACQUAINTED with the restraints of a cloistered year. The primary goal was to become more spiritual, to get in touch with the Divine within us. We had longer hours at prayer and no involvement with the secular world. For some, scrubbing and polishing the novitiate and refectory floors and windows until they shone replaced taking care of the children.

Sister Malachy's kitchen, where I spent my postulant year, wasn't exactly in the secular category, but because there was a chance I might listen to Irish music when cleaning the priests' house, I was taken off that job.

"Lash into it," Sister Malachy said when I asked about playing records in the priests' house while she and I cleaned during the previous year.

"It doesn't seem right that we Sisters should be cleaning and cooking for the priests," I said. "Why doesn't the diocese hire someone to take care of them if they can't do it themselves?"

"Well, you're right of course," she laughed. "But it's part of the hierarchy of things. So we'll say no more about it. But, listen, Father O' Connor has a good music collection. Put on that record of Mary O Hara's harp music. It'll do the both of us good. If we're going to clean his house free of charge, the least we can have is a bit of music."

But Mother Mistress didn't agree that music would be a good idea during novice year. So I was assigned to clean the stairs that led to the trunk room instead. It was a terribly boring charge, sweeping stairs every day, but I tried to "offer it up," as my mother would say when we couldn't have what we wanted. "Let ye offer it up for the sins of the world." This concept made no sense to me, but I thought it might have helped someone who was wronged, maybe someone who had too many children that she couldn't care for.

Shortly after reception as novices, a rumor surfaced that Mother Mistress was about to announce some unpleasant discipline. Mariella found out when visiting one of the junior professed nuns that it was something "huge." That was as much as she knew. Some of the novices quizzed me, thinking that Mag would have filled me in, but of course she hadn't.

"Just because Mag is now a professed nun doesn't mean she's told me about novitiate rules," I was tired of explaining.

Mag had gone back to her mission in Philadelphia after attending the ceremony for my reception day. I felt somewhat relieved that she had shared the fact that she was due to go to the hospital for evaluation soon. "If I can't be near you, at least I can pray," I had said.

As to the new mysterious practice, Mariella told us that it was rumored to be even worse than cutting our hair. So once again we waited our turns in the workroom and were called into Mother Mistress's office one by one. Each one in turn came out of the office clutching a little black silk bag and looking nervous as she hurried straight into the dimly lit chapel to sit in silence. Those of us waiting our turns looked at each other gobsmacked. No one, not even Mariella, who never kept the silence, talked.

Finally, my turn came. I knocked, gave the salutation, "Praised be Jesus Christ," knelt, kissed Mother Mistress's scapular, and remained kneeling. The brown linoleum floor held my eyes. My hands were under my scapular with thumbs tucked in the cord around my waist. I became aware of a pain in the back of my neck. The squeaky sound of Mother Mistress opening her desk drawer was a relief. My mind focused on her instead of my pain.

Mother Mistress, standing upright, seemed to tower above me where I knelt. She always seemed so tall when I knelt at her feet. But now she seemed taller than usual.

She extended a little black silk bag with a drawstring that was tied tightly. When I reached to take it, she untied an identical black bag revealing a footlong silver chain. The links, about a half-inch in diameter, dangled from her hand in front of my face.

"This is 'the discipline,' Sister."

"The discipline?" My stomach was feeling queasy.

"Sit down, Sister, before you fall down."

I flopped onto the chair near the door.

"This chain, you will keep with you always to remind you to avoid sins of the flesh. You will use it on the first Friday of each month."

With open mouth, I nodded my head and then closed the bag. I thought that if I acted as if I knew what she was talking about, I suddenly somehow miraculously *would* know.

"It's to beat yourself, Sister."

"To beat..."A look of horror came over my face. I could feel my eyes widening as my head jerked backwards. I must have looked like someone in a dentist's chair about to have surgery without novocaine. I stood up halfway and moved the chair away from her desk.

"Just calm yourself, Sister."

Calm myself? I had one hand on the door. I must have been thinking of escape.

"Now, Sister, there's no need for hysteria. The novices and professed nuns who live at the motherhouse perform the discipline together on first Fridays. When the lights are turned out, we lift our habits to beat ourselves on the thighs while we pray the *'De Profundus.'"*

"Oh my God," I said.

"Please do not to take God's name in vain," she said.

The following Friday, we novices were more giddy than usual.

"Watch out for sins of the flesh," Mariella mimicked using Mother Mistress's tone.

"Is she nuts or what?" Brigid asked. "No one is going to beat themselves."

Although I agreed that this, indeed, was nuts, I also thought it must be a means of moving forward. I was serious about becoming holy, and if this is what it took, then so be it. After all, I reasoned, our founder, St. Francis, used this discipline to keep sins of the flesh at bay.

But the thing was, I hadn't had any so-called impure thoughts since I became a novice. Getting used to the habit and starched white veil, to say nothing of the segolia that gave me headaches, was enough to banish any thoughts of a sexual nature. It seemed ages since the end of postulant year, when I saw the man who came in to fix the window in the workroom. He was tall, handsome, and blond. We were not allowed in the workroom while he worked, but I saw him out of the corner of my eye as he turned the corner by the chapel, his arse tight in his overalls, his shoulders broad as he walked with a stride that caused a pleasant sensation to creep over my breasts and further south. I felt giddy and wished I were dusting or sweeping the workroom where he was fixing the window.

I knew I'd feel that sensation again whenever a handsome man happened to come into my life. What would happen when I took my vows and went out to work among seculars? It must be what the discipline is for, I thought. It will prepare me for fighting temptation. I prayed and fretted that I'd get over the disgust I felt at the thought of this act of beating myself.

When we filed out of chapel on the first Friday and neared the hallway of Sacred Heart Hall, the entire community of novices and professed nuns began to chant the "De Profendus." The lights went out, just as Mother Mistress said, and a bell rang. The last time I'd heard the death bell was on reception day, when we became brides of Christ and were covered with the black shroud. As the prayer continued, the jingle of chains caused sweat to form under the linen band that covered my forehead. It ran into my eyes, making them sting.

I took my little bag off my cord where it was tied at my waist, fumbled with the string in the dark and felt the coolness of the chain in my hand. I thought perhaps the chant would be finished by the time I was ready to start, but it went on and on. Suddenly, I threw the chain back into its little black bag and tied it back on my cord. It felt right to do that. I didn't ask any of the others what they did, but years later, when we discussed this archaic practice, friends agreed that they, too, gave the discipline a miss.

Another mortification practice we were introduced to during novice year was eating off the floor on Good Friday. Chairs were removed from the refectory, and instead of setting the tables we "set the floor." This meant arranging the place settings one behind the other on the shiny green and white linoleum tiles.

"Skip a tile, Sisters. Leave room for the feet of the sister who kneels in front of you," Mother Mistress directed. Because we ate kneeling, it was more than a bit disturbing to see someone's shoes so close to my plate. Because the dish of fish and vegetables was too hot to hold, I kept it on the floor. I could see shoulders moving up and down in fits of giggles and felt confused that I didn't believe this act of humility and mortification was going to be of any more benefit than the discipline was in deepening my spirituality.

The forty hours devotion, when we took turns kneeling in front of the altar in adoration of the Blessed Sacrament, was more meaningful. We were each assigned an hour at a time to watch and pray. This was in commemoration of the night before His death, when Christ asked the apostles to watch and pray with Him. During this time of adoration, I felt close to God, felt He was inviting me to be with Him, and I believed I was truly loved by Jesus.

"If the apostles couldn't stay awake, why do we have to?" Brigid laughed good-naturedly. She was not an early morning person. Neither was Louisa, who was often corrected for being late to prayers. To help her overcome this fault, Louisa had the job of ringing the bell to wake us in the morning. We laughed when she told us at recreation how she had to duck a few slippers that came flying from behind curtained beds in the wee hours of Holy Week.

If it weren't for bouts of silliness, our cloistered novice year would have been difficult to bear. Mariella helped by coming up with jokes and pranks to make us laugh and keep Mother Mistress on her toes.

On one occasion, Mariella was dusting a life-sized statue of the Sacred Heart of Jesus at the entrance to the dormitory. When she realized the arms of the statue were removable, she took them off, dusted them and hid them in the communal Kotex bin. Donna, a very excitable, nervous type, went to get a pad. When she took the lid off the bin and saw the two arms complete with wounds on the hands reaching up to her, she screamed so loud and so long that several novices crowded into the bathroom to see what was wrong.

I was sometimes annoyed with myself for finding enjoyment in distractions such as these. How was I ever going to reach perfection if I didn't work harder at avoiding distractions? Trying to accept the humiliating remarks of Mother Mistress as she tried her best to make me humble was a challenge. When I volunteered to read in "the box," a sort of pulpit in the refectory where novices read spiritual books aloud for the edification of the community during meals, she looked at me in horror.

"Really, Sister, have you listened to yourself speak? What would the Sisters think of me if they couldn't understand you?"

When I responded with a look of confusion, she said, "You know you have an accent?"

I got up from my knees. I couldn't challenge her in that submissive position. I knew it was against the rules, but I went ahead.

"What's wrong with my accent, Mother Mistress?"

I really wanted to tell her about being nominated for the Miss Voice and Courtesy Award at the phone company, but that would only make her worse, I decided. Still, I wanted an answer to the question of my accent.

"I know you mean well and that you don't mean to question

authority, Sister. But, the community would not be edified if they couldn't understand the reader." Then she walked away.

I thought that her mean-spiritedness was truly a test from God. I decided if I could manage to respect her position and not hate her, I would surely reach spiritual heights. I prayed daily that I might be able to see Christ in this woman.

One of the novices said that Mother Mistress was suffering from menopause issues. And, indeed, she did spend time in the hospital towards the end of my novice year, so I was more or less able to forgive her. ᘓ

CHAPTER 17

First Mission

*I*T WAS THE END OF SUMMER, 1964, and our novice year was coming to a close. The poles up and down the refectory were covered with typed lists. The heading on each of these lists was the name of a convent, along with its location and the name of the Mother Superior in charge. Beneath the headings were the names of Sisters assigned to that particular convent or mission for the coming September. Novices and professed nuns rushed around, veils flying and cords swinging, frantically looking for their names. A few senior nuns sat quietly, as if they were afraid to find out, waiting for friends to give them the good or bad news.

The year before, as a postulant, I barely noticed these lists as I went about with the others cleaning up after breakfast and going off to help out at Sister Malachy's kitchen and the priests' house. But now it was different. My name was somewhere on one of those lists. I was about to take my first vows and exchange my white veil for a black one.

"Each year at this time, every Sister in the community must pack her trunk and be ready to go wherever God sends her," said Mother Mistress. "You newly professed must be ready, too. It's the mark of a good religious to be prepared to go and do God's will wherever she is sent."

I wondered why so much time should be wasted packing the trunk again if one's assignment didn't change. But that's the way it was. It was a combination of two vows—poverty, because you weren't supposed to be attached to any person or any place, and obedience, because you should always be ready to go where you're sent. Through visits with professed nuns who had been either sponsors or high school teachers, some novices learned about the personalities of the Mother Superiors on the various missions. I had not listened to the gossip, so I felt reasonably calm.

Brigid was frozen at one of the poles. She pointed to a list with one hand and covered her mouth with the other. I went to see what she was so upset about.

"Would you look at this? Oh no," she said, putting her hand back over her mouth.

The name of the Mother Superior on the list she was pointing at, with her own name at the bottom, was none other than our own Mother Mistress—Sister Veronica.

"She's being *changed,* and I'm in her convent. Can you believe this? How unlucky can I get?" Brigid's voice was hysterical, and the rest of us gathered around her.

"Oh my God," said Mariella. "You're going to be living with Mother Mistress *again.* Oh, you poor thing."

We noticed how pale Brigid was getting.

"Calm down, Mariella," Beatrice said.

"It could be worse," I said. "As my mother would say, 'The devil you know is better than the one you don't.'"

"Not in this case!" Brigid yelled. Everyone agreed. We all broke the rules and hugged Brigid as we tried to say something to make her feel better.

"Don't forget, we'll be going to Ladycliff to study on Saturdays," Mariella reminded her. "And we'll all see each other."

"Except me," I moaned. "I can't go to Ladycliff. Don't forget I have more high-school subjects to do."

"I'd gladly switch with you," Brigid said. "Oh my God, anyone want to switch with me?"

"As if that's an option," said Louisa.

I went from pole to pole looking for my name. Finally, I found it on the list for Saint Joseph's Convent, Bogota, New Jersey. To my amazement, I was assigned a kindergarten class. Me? I still didn't know what an amoeba was, and I couldn't do math.

"How can I be a teacher? I need to study. This must be a mistake," I said out loud.

"Let's see what you got, Maura." Mariella was bustling about, checking all our lists. She had the "inside scoop" on several of the superiors, and I was afraid of what she was going to tell me about mine.

"She's tough. I have to tell you, they say Sister Brenda is a tough cookie. I heard she's real bossy. But if she likes you, you're all set. Otherwise, forgedaboutit."

"Don't tell me any more, Mariella."

"But who knows? She may be getting mellow in her old age," she concluded.

"Thanks," I said. "You're a big help. If she's tough, I'll be done in. How can I possibly be a teacher?"

"Just think of your American-history teacher, Sister Mary Andrew. No matter what you do, you won't fall asleep in the classroom."

I had to laugh and agree in spite of my building anxiety.

Louisa's assignment was with teenage girls in the Bronx, but she was calmer than most because of her experience helping out with teens during postulant year.

"The worst part of it is that we're all going to be separated," she said. "Look, every convent has just one of our names at the bottom of these lists."

I began to feel a twinge of sadness. Ten unknown nuns and a bossy Mother Superior would replace Louisa's calmness, Brigid's vivaciousness, Mariella's humor, and Beatrice's positive attitude. Cindy was going to be a high school teacher. "Because of you, I've had a bit of practice," she reminded me. I wished her well and said I hoped she wouldn't have any farm girls refusing to dissect frogs in her class.

I wished I felt more spiritual that morning. I wondered if I was really doing God's will. It was as if there had been no novice year, no practicing forgetting about the world, no leaving everything in God's hands. Although our habits were medieval dress, we were still a group of young women, going off to new posts, worrying about doing a good job and pleasing the boss, I thought. The other difference, of course, was that we would be working for an institution—the Church—and we would not get paid. In spite of Mother Mistress's constant warnings to never touch another Sister, we hugged each other. Plenty of tears were shed. Everyone vowed to stay in touch.

"We'll see each other at Ladycliff on Satudays. We'll catch up then," Brigid yelled through her tears. She took off her granny glasses and dried her eyes.

"Good thing we still have college courses to finish," Louisa added, "or we'd really miss each other."

I still had to pass a high school math course before I could apply for acceptance at Ladycliff College. I had more practice with separation anxiety than the rest of them. I reminded myself that I managed to get through leaving Ireland. Not seeing my band for a while couldn't be as hard as that, I decided.

Mother Mary Brenda, a short, fat nun with a face that alternated between smiles and severity, kissed my segolia-clad cheeks as she welcomed me to Saint Joseph's. It was as though I were her long lost daughter finally returned. I couldn't believe it. She enthusiastically waved me inside to the dining room where the other Sisters were lined up, also ready with a kiss on my segolia.

The younger nuns hurried into the kitchen and brought forth all manner of cakes, cookies and pies. I couldn't believe this celebration was to welcome *me*. I kept looking around to see if there were any signs of a birthday or graduation decorations, but the sign on the dining room door said, "Welcome Sister Maura."

I tried to remember everyone's name when they introduced themselves around the table. When they asked where I came from in Ireland, I knew my accent showed. I was ready for Sister Brenda to announce that the Kindergarten class was a mistake, that I would be in charge of the kitchen or laundry or something. She'd tell me the list was wrong, that someone with a degree will teach Kindergarten, I thought. I would be relieved. I wasn't ready to do something I knew nothing about anyway.

I was surprised when she spoke with a slight touch of an Irish accent herself. "I hope you like to work, Sister. There's a lot to be done in school. Sister Anne will show you where your classroom is."

Panic again. It's true. I'm to be a teacher. But how? I didn't want to say that I was scared because that would show I was weak and didn't have faith that God would see me through.

"I'll do the best I can, Mother," I said without much conviction in my voice.

Sister Anne was the eighth-grade teacher. She had a plump face and a ready smile. Apart from the elderly Sister Miriam, who reminded me of Sister Mary Andrew, Anne was the oldest in the house. She took me to the classroom and assured me she was available if I needed help.

"Help? I don't know anything."

"We all started out not knowing much. You'll be fine."

"But I have had no college courses. The only American classroom I've ever been in is the one in the novitiate. I know nothing about children, much less teaching. What do I do?"

She showed me the textbooks and the closet where the supplies were kept. She encouraged me to visit the first-grade room. To my surprise, the first-grade teacher, Sister June Marie, the most junior sister in the house until I arrived, was not friendly. I noticed earlier that she had not welcomed me as warmly as the others had. A tiny, frail looking nun, she wore thick glasses that intensified her perplexed brown eyes.

"Well, I've got work to do," she said as she went back to cutting out letters from construction paper. "Talk to Mother Brenda if you have any questions."

"Mother Brenda gives her a hard time," Anne said later. "She's nervous most of the time, but she's a good teacher."

"Why does Mother give her a hard time?"

"Oh, I don't know. June is always late for prayers, but I wish Mother would ease up on her sometimes."

My seat was next to Sister June's in the dining room. She passed the food but never spoke to me during dinner. What a difference from Brigid, Louisa, Mariella and the others. I really missed them. Well, this was a trial, I decided. She was placed here as a trial for me. At least Mother Mistress was right about trials in convent life.

When June Marie was late for morning prayers, she had to perform "the bow." This practice was obsolete on most missions, but Mother Brenda insisted upon it because she said it was important to be on time for prayers. When a tardy Sister performed the bow, she knelt in the middle aisle of the chapel, bowed facing the altar until her face almost touched the floor, stood up straight, bowed from the waist, turned to the community, bowed again to the right and then the left. I always thought the bow was distracting in the novitiate and expected the chapel to break out in applause whenever it was executed. But here in a smaller community, it was more embarrassing than performance-like. I didn't want to look up when June Marie was late.

One day soon after I arrived, she didn't turn up at all for morning prayers. Mother Brenda sent Anne to look for her. I could hear Anne whisper in the back of the chapel.

"Sister June Marie isn't in her room or anywhere in the convent."

That evening, the police were interviewing Mother Brenda.

"It seems that June has had a nervous breakdown," Mother told us at dinner. "She ran away during the night. It's so embarrassing. She was found by the police dressed in her robe and slippers trying to make her way on foot to the motherhouse in Peekskill."

Shortly afterward, we found out she left the order. I felt sad realizing that she must have been under tremendous strain. I wondered if she might have had a secret lover out there somewhere. Maybe her health broke down because she wanted to be with him?

After June left, Mother Brenda became a dictator. She started to read our mail, both incoming and outgoing. I had been used to that practice in the novitiate, when our opened letters were placed on the workroom table, but I knew it was unusual for this practice to continue on the missions.

"This isn't appropriate, Sister," Mother Brenda said. She was holding a letter I had written to my parents. "Rewrite it, and don't use those Irish expressions."

"You mean 'slán' instead of 'goodbye'? But I always say 'slán.'" I was shocked that she would find fault with my using a word in the Irish language.

"You should finish your letter with, 'In the love of Christ.'"

I handed in the corrected letter to her, but wrote another one to exchange before I mailed it.

Although she was dictatorial in the convent, Mother Brenda was a supportive school principal. She encouraged teachers to help each other and didn't interfere unnecessarily with teachers' ideas and practices.

"All of you help Sister Maura. Remember when you were starting out," she said at the meeting before school opened.

The second-grade teacher, Sister Helena, took me under her tutelage, showing me what she had done in her room and making suggestions as to what I might do for kindergarten students. When she was finished decorating her classroom, she helped me with mine. When Mother Brenda came to check on how I was getting on, she was pleased. She handed me my list of students.

"You'll have fifty-three in the morning Kindergarten class and fifty in the afternoon class. Make sure they all learn, and if you need help at any time, ask for it." She left me then and went to give a list of names to the next teacher.

I froze where I was, standing with my mouth open. I went to my desk and tried to imagine fifty-three five-year-olds sitting around the tables in the room. A small bird alighted on the windowsill and then flew off. Francis was trying to show me that God would take care of me, I thought. Still, I said aloud, "I can't do this." In a few days, I'd have one hundred and three students, and I had no clue what to do with them. How could I be a teacher? I felt like a fraud.

I should talk to Mother Brenda, I thought. She is, after all, the principal of the school. I should tell her I am not going to be able to teach all those five-year-olds. I should simply say I don't know what to do. Instead I went to chapel and asked God's help.

"Dear God, You who know all things, help me with this job You have given me to do. I'm frightened."

I sat still. I could feel my face relax. A peace came over me, and I began to feel stronger. The thought came to my mind that God was listening, helping me. "I *can* do this work," I declared, and immediately felt braver for just having said it. ∽

CHAPTER 18

BECOMING AN AMERICAN

THE MORNING CLASS HAD THREE CRIERS.
Between sobs, Joey said he wanted to go back home
and watch Tom and Jerry. Two girls joined in the
chorus—Jennifer and Jan, who were best friends. When one
cried, the other joined in sympathy. They both backed up Joey's
complaint that it wasn't fair they should have to sit there looking
at someone wearing strange clothes.

"Why do you have that black hat on your head?"

"Mommy said I'm not supposed to ask you this, but why do you
wear the same clothes every day?"

I told them "the hat" was called a veil and the clothes were a
kind of uniform.

"Oh, yeah, like a school uniform?"

I thought I was doing great.

When I read them a story about St. Francis, Joey stopped crying
because he had something to tell me.

"That saint would be mad at my brother, 'cause he threw my
fish down the toilet."

"I'm really sorry to hear that," I said, wondering how I was going
to stop the flow of complaints about offending siblings that St.

Francis should know about. I decided it was time to start practicing standing when someone entered the room. Sister Geraldine had told me the first rule in teaching was to have the students stand to greet the principal whenever she visited the class.

"Even if the students are busy working?"

"Yes. And that goes for anyone who enters your classroom. They should stand, greet the visitor, and wait for you to tell them to be seated. Start practicing right away."

And so I did.

"Let's pretend I'm the principal, boys and girls. I'll go out in the hall. When I come in again, you're to stand quietly and say, 'Good morning, Mother Brenda.' Are you ready?"

"Yes, Sister."

After practicing a few times, the next item on the program was lining up table by table so there wouldn't be any pushing to get in line for coats. That procedure took longer because some decided to be clever. Whenever I'd call out "table two" or "three," they'd insist they were five.

"I'm five. My birthday was Saturday."

"Me, too. I'm five."

This distracted the criers enough to stop the whimpering and allow me to read "Goldilocks and the Three Bears."

When the principal finally did grace us with a visit, I was expecting a shuffle of chairs and a burst of voices, but no one stood. I looked around the class, lifting my hands, gesturing for them to stand. Silence.

"Good morning, Mother Brenda," I mouthed. Nothing. I tried again. Time for a bit of acting, I decided. Door open, out I go, in again.

"Good morning, Mother Brenda." There was great enthusiasm in their voices.

The principal laughed. Later, she complimented me.

"You, Sister, are a born teacher. Sister Anne tells me you're worried about not having a teaching degree."

"Well, yes. I..."

"Forget it for now. Just work and follow your natural instincts. You have a gift. Believe you me, there are people with degrees as long as your arm who can't teach."

That evening, I couldn't focus on prayers. Her compliment on my "gift" made my day. It was almost as good as when I was nominated for the Voice and Courtesy Award at the telephone company. They had put my photo on the bulletin board and held a special luncheon for the girls who were nominated.

I knew the training and success at the telephone company played a part in building my self-esteem as a prospective teacher. A nun was not supposed to feel proud, but I couldn't help it. I was excited about the ease with which I followed the Teacher's Guide. Besides, I was having fun with the challenge of getting to know my students.

While the principal was pleased and impressed with my progress as a teacher that year, she was not at all happy that one of her staff was not yet an American citizen.

"The parents are complimenting me on the fine job you're doing with their children, and I'm pleased about that. But, Sister, it's not flattering to the school's image when one of the teachers must register at the post office as an alien resident of the United States. This is your seventh year in the country now, so you are eligible to apply for citizenship."

For some reason, this was not a venture I considered. I was happy registering at the post office every year until I was ready. I was not yet prepared to deny Ireland. I read that when you became a citizen, you must deny your country of birth. In spite of the fact that on profession day I took a vow of poverty, liberating myself from worldly possessions, I was still attached to Ireland emotionally. This was a fault I did not want to rid myself of.

"I'm sure that someday I'll be ready, Mother," I said, hoping she'd think it was an intelligent remark and leave me alone.

"Oh, you're ready now. You've worked four years in the world, spent two in the novitiate, and this is the seventh. I'll ask Sister Anne to be your sponsor. Wait here."

She went downstairs to the kitchen where Anne was cooking. I sat in the community room alone. The others were still in school, correcting papers and planning for the following day. I wished that I, too, were still in school, but my lessons were ready. I wanted to make notes for my upcoming kindergarten graduation ceremonies. I closed my notebook. While I waited, I felt all joy and creativity leave me. I wanted to be an American someday, but I did not want to deny Ireland.

Anne came rushing into the community room with a book. It was about becoming a citizen, she said. She was delighted for me.

"Study this. They'll ask questions about American history and politics. You'll need to know about what's going on right now, Martin Luther King winning the Nobel Peace Prize and everything."

On May 28, 1965, at the courtroom in Hackensack, I sat next to a Chinese man who was still being coached in English while waiting his turn to be called.

"My name is Qxe Chan. I am from Hong Kong. The president of United States is Lyndon Johnson. I will be good citizen of United States."

"Practice that again," his coach said.

"He doesn't even speak English, and he's applying for citizenship. I don't know why you look so worried," Anne said in an encouraging way.

"I'm not worried about the test. I'm worried about my state of mind," I told her.

"But everyone becomes a citizen sooner or later," she smiled.

"I was thinking of later."

"That's the thing with convent life," she said. "You never know when your vow of obedience will be challenged."

I knew she was trying to be helpful, but I did not feel consoled. I did not feel ready for this new step.

After our fingerprints were taken, we were called in alphabetical order. I looked around and noticed the other people, wondering why they looked so happy when I felt miserable. Here with these other immigrants who were ready for this step, I felt no bond. They freely made up their minds to do this, but I did not. I tried to pray, but could only feel anger that the vow had put me in this predicament before I was ready.

They took my photo, and I was asked the name of the president and some other simple questions. When Anne and I got back to the convent, there were congratulatory greetings from everyone. The dining room was decorated in red, white and blue, with streamers and balloons. The table was spread with cheese, wine, and pastries. The priests and some members of the parish had been invited. I was the guest of honor, but I felt miserable.

I ran upstairs to the bathroom and vomited. I took out the letter that stated my certificate of naturalization would be mailed. My eyes stared at one line: "Country of *Former* Nationality." The word "Ireland" had been filled in by the clerk. I quickly put it in a drawer of my desk and went back to the celebration. That night, when I brushed my teeth, I did not want to look at my image in the tiny mirror over the sink. ᒧ

CHAPTER 19

THE BOYS' HOUSE

$\mathcal{I}$ WANTED TO FEEL PROUD to be an American. Instead, I felt like a traitor for having denied Ireland. At the end of that school year, I returned to Peekskill. I missed my kindergarten class terribly but knew that there was no chance to study if I continued at St. Joe's. I felt I was being tested to see what work I should do and if I were flexible enough to be moved whenever and wherever the community was in need. My new mission would allow me to study at Ladycliff, where I would attend college classes on Saturdays. The rest of the week, I would work as a group mother in the institution. When I earned my degree, I would be sent to teach again.

The motherhouse itself was familiar, though the work was not. Because my Irish accent had prevented me from acquiring any knowledge of this job during postulant year ("The children would not understand you, Sister," Mother Mistress had said), I didn't feel prepared for the assignment. I took myself to chapel as I had done the year before and prayed for the necessary grace to do a good job.

I was pleased to learn that Mariella was also assigned to the institution that year. We had lots of chats and laughs about our novitiate years.

"Remember when Mother Mistress had a nervous breakdown during novice year?" Mariella said.

"Is that why she was so strange?"

"Well, we didn't know it then, but I found out she had a touch of the nerves. It must have been us. We drove her nuts."

"Speak for yourself, Mariella," I laughed. "Remember the show we put on to welcome her back when she got out of the hospital?"

"It was a regular Broadway production. We had characters like Old King Cole."

"That was you. We made a throne for you." I said

"Pat was a cowgirl singing 'Madalina Catalina' with her guitar."

"And Brigid?"

"She did a ballet performance. She put a mop on her head and tied it up in a bun. And you, of course, did an Irish dance."

"No, I *wanted* to do an Irish dance. But the director, Beatrice, said that Maureen Cawley was going to sing 'Danny Boy,' so I'd have to think of something non-Irish. I reluctantly did a Japanese dance with a fan. Remember, I wore a fancy bathrobe and a black wig someone had left in the pile for the poor?"

"You sang that song from 'The Mikado.' I remember now," Mariella said while pretending to fan herself with a paper napkin. "You were running around the stage in little quick steps and taking elaborate bows every few seconds. You certainly don't have much opportunity for dancing nowadays. But you'll have plenty of exercise with those boys."

She was right. My position as group mother meant I was responsible for twenty boys between the ages of two and five. I was on duty day and night, except when I was relieved for chapel and an hour of recreation each evening. That was usually spent going for walks or talking with Mariella and other nuns in the community room.

My bedroom was so small that if my mother saw it she'd surely say, "The Lord save us. You couldn't swing a cat in this miserable space." The chest of three drawers that held my underwear and aprons made it necessary to enter the room sideways. The single bed, chair and small lamp table left little space to move around. I hung my two habits and bathrobe on hooks on the back of the door. A small window opened into the children's dormitory. The floral curtain covering this window matched the curtain on the window that opened into a yard where the boys played. Each boy had his own cot with a chair beside it. Each had a locker for his pajamas, bathrobe, and slippers. Each boy kept special memorabilia, such as family photos or toys from home, in a box in his locker. With the help of a donated camera, I put each one's picture and name on his locker. They made frames of their own design with construction paper. Each boy had a wooden toy box made by volunteers and patients of the veterans' hospital. These boxes, complete with names painted on the outside, stored toys donated by charitable organizations.

Carmen, the cleaning lady, scrubbed the unit—living room, playroom, dormitory, and shower room—on a daily basis. She changed the bedclothes once a week. The night watch, a lay woman, was responsible for the entire building—three floors with two groups of twenty-five sleeping boys in each group. Her job was to change bed-wetters, but she didn't always get around to them. More often, it was the group mother who heard the cry of the uncomfortable unfortunate who had wet his bed.

Because I was a light sleeper, I usually heard the plea for a dry sheet before the night watch put in her appearance. I would hurry to put on my black bathrobe and slippers. In the early sixties, before Vatican II, the children weren't supposed to see their group mother without her veil, even if they were half asleep or crying with steam rising from their sheets. It made no sense to waste time putting on a veil when a child was uncomfortable, so I didn't.

Nightmares and sleepwalking were common occurrences. One night, I awoke to hear the creek of the outside door that led to the street. I flung on my bathrobe to follow four-year-old Jose, who didn't seem to feel the cold as he walked in his sleep down the steps outside the building. He was going home, he said.

Five-year-old Patrick cried himself to sleep every night. He

wanted his mom, but his dad told him she was in Heaven. He
didn't like that his dad was drinking the stuff that smelled bad.
But he *had* to drink it, Patrick told me, because he was lonely.
He told me his dad was scared because "Mom had sent herself to
Heaven with pills." Maybe God was mad at her and wouldn't let
her in, he said sadly. I told him I was sure God would welcome
his mom because I felt she didn't really mean to leave Patrick. His
dad was allowed to visit every two weeks, and I cried along with
Patrick when it was time for his dad to leave. I had to pick Patrick
up kicking and screaming to take him from the visiting room back
to the group. Social Services were on the case.

Two brothers, David, five, and Josh, three, had a mom but no
dad. He had been killed in a hit-and-run accident. Their mom had
to be hospitalized to keep her from going where their dad was,
David said. Soon, she'd be better, and then she'd come and take
them home. Did I know when soon was coming? I said no. I let
David help Josh dress every day, and that helped David feel he was
a big boy.

One night I awoke hearing a woman's voice coming from the
dormitory. She was calling out "David, Josh, where are you boys?"

I jumped out of bed and ran into the children's dorm. A tiny
moving light was slowly making its way towards me. The sound of
my bedroom door had stopped the voice calling out, but the light
kept moving slowly in the dark. I turned on the hall lights. In the
shadows near the window, a woman was crouched, her head bowed.
When I got closer, a lighted match in her hand showed tears running
down her face. My first response was fear. I blew out the match.

What if she has a weapon? I thought. I grabbed the flashlight
from the drawer in the hallway, and when I turned it on, I could
see she was only partially dressed. One shoe, a dress open down the
front, and her blond hair like dried straw gave her the appearance
of a homeless person.

"Don't burn your hand," I said to the chapped fingers holding
the end of a matchstick. I reached down, drawing her up to her feet
and leading her out into the living room. She carried a shopping

bag full of food—loaves of bread, vegetables and cheese. In the light, I saw a hospital nametag on her wrist.

"I want my boys, David and Josh. This food is for my boys. Are my boys hungry?"

"Your boys are not hungry. I take good care of them," I mumbled.

"I got it in a store when the girl wasn't looking. It wasn't wrong to take it because they wouldn't let me have money, and my boys need the food."

Up until then, I was petrified. Now, I wanted to comfort her but didn't know how. I put my hand on her arm and said again that I was taking good care of her children. I knew Mariella was upstairs with her own group of boys. I hurried out into the hallway where the phone was and buzzed her extension, all the while eyeing the woman.

"I'll call the police," Mariella assured me. Within minutes, she ran downstairs, took the woman by the arm and walked her into the hands of a female officer.

I found several matches on the dormitory floor. The watchman at the boys' house was fired for sleeping on the job. I didn't hear how the woman had escaped from the mental hospital, but it was determined by Social Services and the hospital that David and Josh's mom would not be able to visit her children for several months.

The Bureau of Child Welfare would inform us which children would be allowed to have visitations. While Jennifer, the counselor, took the others for a walk, I'd escort those who were to have visitors to their waiting families. The families sat around a table sharing soda and popcorn provided by our shelter.

When it was time for Nigel to have a visit from his mother, he said, "No! I don't wanna go! No! No! No!" He cried and kicked and would not get dressed. I called Sister Mary, the social worker, who said she'd bring the family over to my unit so that Nigel could visit there in his pajamas, if he didn't want to get dressed. When I told him this news, he flung himself on the floor, kicking and screaming.

"I wanna stay here! I wanna stay here!"

"You can stay here," I said. "You won't be going away from here today. Why don't you want to see your mommy?"

"'Cause she gonna burn me with the hot water. 'Cause that man, he gonna come to our house, and he be givin' my momma bad stuff. Then she don't want me no more."

When Nigel's mother came in, Nigel ran behind me screaming and holding on to my chair. I thought of my brother Tommie running behind me to get out of the way of my mother's blows. I put the memory out of my mind and touched Nigel's head and held his hand tight in mine.

Nigel's mother put her head down on one of the shiny yellow children's tables in the living room where she sat. She started to cry, and I could tell she was sorry for burning her son with boiling water. When Nigel saw this, he stopped crying but did not let go of my chair.

I took him by the hand and slowly walked him to the table where she sat. When she reached for him, he pulled away. The social worker had to tell her to leave, that Nigel would be better prepared to see her next time. Nigel said goodbye with just a little wave. He looked braver by then, but was still backing away, holding on to the bolt of the door that separated him from his mother.

For the next five years, this work was my life—this and my studies at Ladycliff College on Saturdays. My work with the children was at once a heartbreaking and spiritually rewarding experience.

At the beginning of my fourth year there, Mag was transferred from Philadelphia to join our staff at the institution. I thought this would be an opportunity to get to know her better, but that was not to be. ᕦ

CHAPTER 20

Mag Again

$\mathcal{I}$N THE SILENCE AND IN DARKNESS, God
spoke. I fell asleep each night knowing that I was
loved and cared for by The King of Kings. I believed
that in the absence of light, when the bell was rung for night
silence, my mind could more deeply reflect on the presence of God
and the joy and wonder of having been chosen to be His bride.
As such, I was a replacement for those mothers unable to care for
their children. The joy that made me glad to be alive every day
intensified when Mag arrived at the boys' house and was assigned
a group of boys one floor above me. It would be easier for Mag
and me to get to know each other now. I thought this was God's
way of inviting us to learn to appreciate and love each other more.
The stern novitiate rules were a thing of the past, and religious life
was meant to be peaceful and joyous, the way St. Francis of Assisi
meant it to be, I told myself.

I imagined Mag and me writing to our younger sister, Bridie,
together, congratulating her on her plans to marry Séamus, the
good-looking lad from Tipperary she had met working on the
buses in London. Bridie had sent us the wedding announcement.
She said she understood the rules wouldn't allow use to be able to

attend the wedding. This made me sad for all three of us.

The community had just begun to see the wisdom of allowing nuns to attend weddings and funerals. Mag and I, however, would not enjoy this new permission for some time. Home visits for nuns born outside the U.S. had to be planned after Perpetual Vows—seven years of total service. "It's unfair," I had complained to the Mother General when she visited from Rome.

"The life of a dedicated religious has many crosses," she responded.

Neither Mag nor I knew anything about Bridie's life in the U.K. Years later, when Bridie told me about her first experience in London, I was aghast at how much of each other's lives we had missed. I had no idea that she and other young Irish women of the sixties were turned away from digs in London, where the signs read "No Irish, No Blacks, and No Dogs Allowed."

Because we were in the convent, Bridie was embarrassed to write and tell us about her hostile welcome to the city of her dreams. She and her friend Noreen were harassed by the landlady in the rooming house where they lived. Bridie found herself walking down Holloway Road in North London, her parakeet in a cage in one hand, her dilapidated suitcase in the other, and two shillings in her pocket. She was put out of the rooming house because Noreen got pregnant. "You'll likely be next," the landlady said. "I can't take a chance on you lot. You Irish are all alike," she told Bridie.

I opened my trunk in the hallway outside my room and took out the beautiful writing paper with pink rose buds in the upper left-hand corner. This had been a Christmas gift from one of my kindergarten students the year before. Bridie would be pleased and surprised if Mag and I sent her a shared letter of congratulations, I thought.

When the nine o'clock bell rang announcing "The Great Silence," I went upstairs to Mag's room, writing paper in hand. But when I didn't see a light under her door, I didn't knock. She might not be feeling well, I thought. She may have gone to bed early. The next night, I waited for the night watchwoman to finish her rounds in Mag's dormitory. When she shone her flashlight in the direction of the exit, preparing to check the next group of boys, I took a step towards Mag's door and knocked lightly. No answer. "Mag?" I called softly, but there was still no reply. I reluctantly returned to my room.

"Look," I said to the drip that trickled from the rusty faucet into the small sink below the window in my room, "I just wanted to know about your health, what happened in the hospital, and if you have to take medication."

It bothered me terribly that Mag and I were becoming more like strangers, even in the refectory, where it would have been easy for us to talk.

"What's wrong with us? Why can't we visit each other when the boys are asleep?" I said one evening during dinner. I passed her the milk and glared at her.

"We shouldn't break night silence," she said.

"But I want to talk to you about the hospital in Philadelphia. And we need to write to Bridie."

She breathed a deep sigh. I knew she was troubled.

Days and weeks went by. My sister and I would pass each other going to or coming from the boys' house. Mag would always greet me with, "Praised be Jesus Christ." But instead of, "Forever be praised," I often said, "Hi, Mag!" I tried not to think about the fact that we were becoming more and more like strangers, preferring to believe that God would bring us closer. I decided that God had sent this trial to help me find holiness and wisdom.

I had read in some spiritual reading book that physical pain should be considered a gift because it was a means of developing a likeness to Christ. I didn't want physical pain, but neither did I want to admit that I was embarrassed by, and in awe of, Mag. She stood out as being one of those "Saintly Sisters" her contemporaries would avoid because they felt she was "too holy." I remember wishing I hadn't felt complimented when a sister from her band said, "You're so much more natural and lively than your sister. You'd never know you two were blood sisters." The older nuns made comments like, "How well that young Sister is bearing up under the cross of sickness that God has sent her. You must be so proud to be her sister."

There it was. My sister was on the road to sainthood, and I was still envious and competitive, as if we were small girls back home in Mayo.

One evening after supper, Mother Superior called me into her office. She asked if I had talked to Mag lately.

"Not really," I said.

"Your sister is leaving us. She is returning to the world."

"Leaving?" I could feel the color drain from my face as I shook my head from side to side. I slowly got up from the chair and backed away from her. The mixture of sadness and anger that welled up in me as I rushed from her office was overwhelming. I hurried to Mag's unit in the boys' house. The word "loss" wasn't strong enough for the feeling I had.

I found Mag in her room, dressed in her black bathrobe and slippers. She was putting her two habits, veils and aprons into her trunk. A plain, blue, A-line cotton dress hung on the back of her door.

"It's God's will I must go. Besides, I'm not well physically, and the strain of living this life is becoming too much."

When I put my arms out, we held each other and both cried. I felt she was real then. Mag gestured towards the blue dress she had found at the front office in the pile for the poor.

"I have to change into this at the Kennedy Home in the Bronx tomorrow, because, of course, I must wear my habit when I leave here," she said while taking the habit she had just packed out again and hanging it over the blue dress.

"Will you stay with Anne, your old friend from Dublin?"

"Yes. I wrote Anne. She'll pick me up at The Kennedy Home, help me get dressed and make sure I look presentable."

"I'll visit you and you'll visit me and we'll be friends," I said. We hugged each other again.

After she left, I missed her so much that, for a while, I resented Sally, the young nun who took over Mag's group of boys. But as time wore on, I was struck by the freedom I felt by not being in competition with her anymore.

After a while, Mag's health seemed to improve. She even started dating. The relief for me was such that I stopped worrying about becoming holy and decided that God would take care of my rate of progress in His own time. ☙

CHAPTER 21

The Modern Habit

*T*HE SECOND VATICAN COUNSEL (Vatican II) was at this time dealing with relations between the Church and the modern world. It was also addressing ecumenism and relations with other religions. In keeping with the mandates of Vatican II, our community formed a committee to research and make suggestions for a more modern, practical habit. Whatever it was going to look like, it had to meet the *Perfectae Caritatis'* prescribed requirements of health and be "suited to the circumstances of time and place, and to the needs of the ministry involved."

The committee members and associates designed and made models of new habits to be voted upon. A "fashion show" was held on the stage of the auditorium at Ladycliff College. The community came together to view the styles and vote on an appropriate "modern" habit.

The sisters on the committee, who showed the styles, were of various sizes and ages. A perfect size eight, I had a vision of myself showing the smart, knee-length one with three-quarter sleeves and narrow scapular that fastened at the sides with loops. However, since most members of the community were a few sizes larger, I knew I wasn't a practical choice as a model.

The modeling—walking across the stage while one of the committee members gave a brief description at the mic—was for us a most usual experience. The mid-calf look, which allowed for the partial showing of legs, resulted in a few gasps from senior members in the audience. This must have influenced the Sister about to show the knee-length habit because she never appeared on stage. The conservative nuns were offended. They did not like this edict from Rome. On the way out of the hall, there were murmurs of dissatisfaction.

"Mark my words. Things will get out of hand."

"You said it, Sister. Vanity will most certainly creep in, and who knows where all this modern-day style will lead?"

Those elected as delegates to the chapter on renewal knew that change would come slowly for some. The segolia and the foot-long crucifix that hung from a buttonhole over the chest were first to go. The segolia didn't meet the requirements of the health criteria on account of its tightness around the head, neck and ears. A medieval garment, it didn't fit time and place, either. The crucifix was hazardous to health because of its weight over the left breast. It was accused by some of causing cancer. My objection to it as a group mother was that it was so heavy, so clumsy, that if you didn't remember to hold or move it aside when bending down to help a child tie a shoe, the unfortunate child might get a bang on the head.

The delegates determined that apart from the segolia and crucifix, changing to a shorter habit should be optional. As a result, those who preferred the long look continued wearing it with the new modified veil. Some of the older members opted for the new mid-calf habit, and a few younger ones chose to keep the long one. Perhaps they decided this would be less of a threat to their vow of celibacy.

My first day wearing this new habit in the boys' house, I tried looking at myself in the two-foot-long mirror at the end of the lockers in their dormitory. I could only see from my waist down. My dancer's legs hadn't changed. I had used a portion of the forty-dollar-a-month allowance that we now received as part of the new changes to buy pantyhose. (Before, we used black cotton stockings.) The allowance was meant for recreation, such as theater and buying gifts or small toiletries.

"Imagine not having to ask for toothpaste or soap anymore. I can now buy my own," I had written in a letter to Mag. She wrote back saying she was flabbergasted by the changes, recalling how she left the convent in the dress she found in a pile for the poor.

My new, mid-calf habit was a simple A-line dress with three-quarter length sleeves. The scapular was optional. It was fastened at the sides by loops buttoning the front to the back. The material was a lighter blend of wool and a lighter shade of gray than the old habit. The veil was shoulder-length and was attached to a black cap, which fit comfortably and showed the hair in front. Variations on this style were also approved so that, later, skirts and blouses were also worn with and without the veil.

On this first day appearing in my new habit, I scrunched down in front of the mirror above the tiny sinks in the boys' bathroom, to see if my hair was in place. I was overjoyed seeing my hair again. I opened the blind to see the effect in daylight. March was on its way out, and the rain was pelting against the window with no sign of allowing the sun to help with my vanity.

Smiling at my new image in the mirror, I adjusted my veil. With this new look, I hoped it wouldn't be long until it was decided that mirrors would be useful. Until then, I'd have to settle for this one above a tiny sink in the bathroom. I remembered five years earlier when my hair had been all cut off in the novitiate. How sad I had felt watching the auburn curls fall to the floor.

I stayed hunched there on the tiled floor for several minutes, admiring my modern look. The new veil was light on my head. It felt wonderful to be free of the segolia, not feel it wrapped around my neck. My entire face was free again.

The seven o'clock bell rang. It was time to wake the boys. What in the world would they think? I should have tried to prepare them the night before but couldn't think of what to say. Explaining Vacitan II's *Perfectae Caritatis* to boys under five would be a challenge. Some of the five-year-olds, who had come from The Foundling Home in New York City when they were only two, had been in my group for three years. They were used to seeing me in the long habit with the crucifix dangling from the buttonhole on the left side of the scapular—the same look day in and day out. Sometimes they'd ask me if Sisters had hair and necks, or if I was too hot in summer in my "big clothes."

When I turned on the dormitory light, those who were early risers were already awake.

"Oooooh. You got legs."

"Look, look. Sister Maura got legs."

Little pajama-clad lads rubbing the sleep from their eyes stood still and stared.

"Where you got the new hair, Sister?"

"Yeah. You gots hair."

"Why you have new clothes?"

"What you did wit your old clothes?"

They were all talking at once and crowding around me. Some were reaching up, trying to touch my hair. One was insisting that my hair was new, that I must have bought it in the store.

"You dumb. Nobody gets hair in the store," another countered.

"She didn't got hair before. How come she gots it now?"

I laughed, enjoying their comments, but decided it was time to get some quiet and order. I didn't want Sister Imelda, still in a long habit, screaming at us for being late to breakfast.

"Now, boys, some of the Sisters are going to be wearing new clothes like this—starting today."

"You mean like Easter?"

"No. Yes."

"Yay! Today is Easter. Today is Easter!"

"No, no. Today is not Easter."

Some had already run into the living room to look for Easter baskets.

"The Easter Bunny, he forgot to come. It's not Easter?"

"No. In a few weeks it will be Easter."

"But why you gots new clothes if it ain't Easter?"

"Yeah, and new hair?"

Finally, I said that the Sisters got tired of the old clothes and wanted to wear new ones so they wouldn't be so hot, that it would be easier to play ball in the new clothes.

"Oh, you can run faster with the new clothes."

"Right. It will be more fun to run and play ball with you now."

"Yay!"

There, I thought. I've covered "requirements of health" and "needs of ministry." ᗡᴄ

CHAPTER 22

Perpetual Vows

"DO YOU FEEL READY, SISTER?" asked the new Mother Provincial. She looked at me with warm inquiring eyes as she emerged from behind the uncluttered mahogany desk with its vase of bright daffodils. We sat facing each other near the window, overlooking the Hudson River.

When I considered her question, my mind flashed to the calm I felt when, with controlled voice, I knelt on the altar steps to renew my temporary vows once every year for the past six years: "I, Sister Maura Angela of The Missionary Sisters of Saint Francis, renew my vows of poverty, chastity and obedience—for one year…I ask God and the intercession of the Virgin Mary the grace of faithful observance of these my holy vows."

But now it was time to decide if these vows should continue as impermanent for one more year or become perpetual—a life of commitment. What decision would I make? That's what Mother Provincial was asking me.

"Well, Mother, at this moment, as I sit here in this office, religious life feels right to me. But if in the future, I—"

"There is only the present," she interrupted me. "We don't know what tomorrow brings. What we do know is…." She reached over and gently patted my hand. "What we know is, if we follow the life that God has planned for us, we will be happy."

That makes sense, I thought. We do not know the future. And if I feel at the moment that this is the life I should live, then I must live it.

My thoughts flashed to the members of my dwindling band. The last of those with whom I had bonded to leave was Mariella. The night before she left, we reminisced about the others.

Louisa was married and living somewhere in the Boston area. Brigid, who had left shortly after we changed to the modern habit, wrote to tell us she had been to a hair salon. "As soon as my sister Gerri picked me up at the convent in the Bronx, I told her, 'Take me to the hairdresser, for God's sake. I want to make an appointment to look normal again.'"

"Let's keep in touch, Maura," Mariella said with a hug. I would remind myself years later how she predicted that we'd have reunions and talk about our novitiate days with Mother Mistress.

"You are one of seven remaining out of the original twenty-eight who entered our community seven years ago," Mother Provincial said. "I see no reason for you to renew another year. If you feel called, you may make the decision to follow by taking perpetual vows." After a moment's pause, she asked, "And how is your sister?"

Mag? Confusion flooded my mind. I wanted to answer with a question of why her predecessor sent Mag home four years earlier—just when I was trying to get to know her. But I told myself again I must not question the action of God's representative.

"It's my understanding that it was because of health reasons she had to leave the order," she said, as if reading my mind. "She was not strong enough for the life."

"I know," I said. But though I knew she was sick, I did not understand, couldn't make myself accept, that she should be dismissed for lack of perfect health. And I felt guilty for the feeling of victory that took over my thoughts. Mag couldn't make it, but I could.

My eyes found the image of Christ crucified hanging on the wall over Mother Provincial's desk. I reminded myself of His sacrifice and returned my gaze to Mother Provincial.

"Yes," I said, "I believe God has called me. I think this is where I belong."

When I left Mother Provincial's office, I acknowledged to myself that the modern habit, although I liked wearing it, was somewhat of a hindrance. Smiles from a male colleague sent sexual tension through my body. I prayed to overcome this challenge to my vocation.

"Tests of the flesh, Sisters. Be vigilant. Remember custody of the eyes…and pray. If this life were easy, it wouldn't be worth the challenge," Mother Mistress used to say.

I prayed. Over and over, I spoke the words of our founder, St. Francis: "'Lord, make me an instrument of your peace…Where there is doubt, faith…." I concluded that my doubts were just the ordinary kind—doubts that, according to the spiritual reading books, women and men in religious life are supposed to have.

We began the eight-day retreat in preparation for perpetual vows by greeting each other on the lawn outside the castle-like convent at Mohegan Lake. Rose bushes lined the walkway leading to the main entrance. The fragrance of newly mown grass in the front lawn was a reminder to me of new beginnings.

The sun, shining through the stained-glass chapel windows, brought floating rainbows extending from the wall to the bench in front of me. I had the sudden urge to move there, so as to be bathed in color. I was hoping for a spiritual experience from the God to Whom I was about to offer my entire life. The clean smell of evergreen and newly mown grass wafting in through the open windows seemed to lift me. I felt at peace.

My mother's words, about not having a care in the world because of my marriage to God, came and went. I wanted to feel that she had nothing to do with my being there. But sometimes during prayer and meditation, I found myself talking to her: "You have no business reminding me that this lifestyle is worry free. What do you know about it? I'll have my share of worries avoiding distractions and temptations."

"Many are called but few are chosen," the retreat priest reminded us several times in the course of the week. He quoted the psalms, the gospels, ecumenical theologians such as Teilhard de Chardin and secular works like Robert Frost's "The Road Not Taken": *Two roads diverged in a wood, and I, I took the one less traveled by, And that has made all the difference.*

As the retreat progressed, the time I spent alone in chapel or walking the beautiful grounds at Mohegan Lake was not always uplifting. At times, I found it difficult to accept that this isolation would bring me holiness. I asked St. Francis to intercede on my behalf, wishing to feel evidence of this concept of being chosen.

There were moments when I felt sure my prayers were answered. Doubts lifted and birds sang—just for me it seemed. At those times, in the quiet of the chapel's candlelight and the scent of flowers, I felt secure. This, I decided, is proof of the presence of God. This deeper awareness of sound and smell must be the pure love of God meant for those who are chosen.

On the final day of the retreat week, I watched a rabbit nibbling on the lawn. When it ran out of sight, I followed along the path to see if I could find its burrow. On a bench, under an oak tree teaming with foliage, a man sat reading. I noticed his clerical collar and realized he was wearing an army uniform. But, mostly, I noticed that he was exceptionally good looking. He stopped reading his breviary, looked up, and smiled as I approached. When he introduced himself, I stepped backwards, tripping over a broken tree branch.

"I'm Father Gray, a chaplain in the Irish army. I'm visiting the U.S. I've just been to West Point to have a look round."

"Welcome to the U.S." I said taking another step away from him, backing into a bench behind me. I was furiously telling myself to regain some dignity and not act like a silly schoolgirl with a crush on a male teacher.

"I believe you Sisters here are on retreat to prepare for perpetual vows. You're brave."

"Brave?"

"Well, religious life is indeed a challenge these days."

I didn't know what to say to make myself feel at ease. The dark green uniform, the tall, slim body, the clerical collar and the sunglasses all made me think he was somehow unreal—a leading man in some romantic film. I thought of Peter Finch in *The Nun's Story*. And for a fleeting moment, I imagined myself as Audrey Hepburn.

"Oh, there's the bell for vespers. Well, nice to meet you," I stammered.

"I'll be here for a couple of days," he called after me. "Maybe someone will invite me to the vow ceremony? I've not been to any modern vow ceremonies in this country."

"Oh, you're invited," I blurted out over my shoulder.

As I hurried off to vespers, I could feel my face burning. I felt it still red as I took my place in chapel. After a while, a calm voice in my head told me that attractive men would simply be obstacles I would have to meet on this road less traveled.

The first reading was taken from *The Vowed Life* by Adrian Van Kaam: "Birth was the first event for which I could not be responsible. No freedom of decision was involved in this. The situation into which I was born is set. By comparison, The Vow signals my birth as a free human being who herself chooses her life orientation. It is a new birth for which I alone am responsible; its consequence will shape my unique destiny...."

I was about to experience this new birth Van Kaam described. Sitting in chapel with the other Sisters, listening to the reading, it was clear to me that, although I felt a tinge of doubt about this step of permanent commitment, I could not see myself in any other life. I had spent seven years preparing myself for this pledge. Still, at this moment, I prayed that if ever I should feel another calling, God would give me the courage to be true to myself.

I closed my eyes and listened to the second reading, taken from the third chapter of St. Paul's letter to the Colossians. The first line of the excerpt began, "You are the people of God; He loved you and chose you for His own."

Mag was in the congregation. I wondered if she envied me. I felt uneasy that such a thought should enter my mind. Cousin Nuala and Uncle Pake were there, too. And way in the back of the chapel was the gorgeous Father Gray. I tried to put him out of my head as fast as I could, but he wouldn't go. There was no doubt God sent this man as some sort of test, I decided. But why am I being tried on the very day I am vowing to give myself to Him forever? God has a peculiar sense of humor. Surely He might have waited and let me have this one day in peace?

I cooled myself down by remembering when I became a novice five years before. I recalled the cold floor under my hands as I lay prostrate. I was glad we had abandoned that ceremony for the sake of future novices. We, a group of five women, had planned this liturgy ourselves instead of taking the lead from Rome. Besides choosing the readings and music, we wrote the vow ceremony and decided that we'd go down the aisle, find our relatives and friends, and hug them at the sign of peace.

When the priest said, "Let us offer each other a sign of peace," we stood, turned, and kissed each other on the cheek. The others shot down the isle to the right and to the left. I had forgotten to tell Mag where to sit, so I didn't know where she was. The first person I saw was Father Gray, way in the back. He was easy to spot in his army uniform. I made a beeline for him and hurriedly kissed his cheek. When I tried to find Mag and the relatives, I noticed the others were all finished with their hugs and kisses and were already on their way back to the altar. "I know Mag is here somewhere," I mumbled, but I was too flustered to search for her. I dashed back to the altar, my face hot and red. What a way to start a vowed life, I thought. I told myself to focus, to find calm and serenity before the priest asked us his questions.

"Sisters, will you share your love with your community in the spirit of Saint Francis, so that together you may be witnesses to Christ's presence with one another within the Church?"

"I will."

"Do you wish to make a permanent commitment to a life of

CALL OF THE LARK * 177

poverty as exemplified by Christ by recognizing the primacy of persons over things, in joyful but non-possessive use of material things and freedom from unwanted dependence upon them?"

"I do wish."

"Are you ready to make a permanent commitment to a life of obedient listening of Christ to all manifestations of the will of His Father in people and events?"

I joined the others in responding.

"Do you wish to make a permanent commitment to a life of chastity, which by its nature liberates the human heart to embrace Christ and mankind?"

"I do wish."

For the act of individual commitment, we stood one by one to pronounce our vows for life. I was nervous but at peace when I spoke.

"In the presence of God and this community, I, Sister Maura Angela Mulligan, vow to God for my whole life, to listen and respond to the Spirit in each person and event through obedience, to share all gifts, both spiritual and material, without hesitation through gospel poverty, to leave myself completely available by sharing with all persons Christ's love for us through chastity according to the rule of the Third Seraphic Order and the constitution of the Franciscan Missionary Sisters, represented by you, Reverend Mother, delegate of the Superior General. I ask of God, through the merits of Jesus Crucified and the intercession of the Immaculate Virgin Mary, the grace of faithful observance of these my holy vows."

The priest responded, "And I receive your vows, and on the part of Almighty God, if you observe them, I promise you everlasting life."

"Amen." ༄

CHAPTER 23

No Child of My Own

FTER FIVE YEARS AS A GROUP MOTHER, some college courses, and a bit of teacher training, the winds of change were calling.

"It's time for you to move on, finish your degree, and return to teaching," said the Reverend Mother. "We know that teaching is your true calling."

In spite of mixed feelings, I was aware that a change was best for me. Sometimes, while trying to study after the boys went to sleep, I'd wake up in the middle of the night, fully clothed with my head in a book.

A week before leaving the boys, I tried to explain that I had to change jobs, go somewhere else—wherever the boss sent me.

"But why you don't wanna stay with us no more?" Trevor asked. He was a tall, dark-skinned boy with sparkling brown eyes and a sharp mind.

"It's not that I don't want to stay with you, Trevor. It's that God wants me to work someplace else now."

I felt foolish having said that. He did not understand. Parents and foster homes had wounded him and the others. Now it seemed I was adding to his pain. I bent down and gathered them in a group hug. Some were starting to cry. I didn't know how to deal with this, and could only trust in divine intervention.

"The life of Sisters like me is different from other grown-ups. We have to do what we're told all the time."

"But," Trevor broke in, leaping up and down. He always jumped excitedly when he figured something out, like the time he got the battery to work on the train set on Christmas morning. "But Sister, you…you can't leave us by ourselves. That's why the police took me and my brother away from our apartment and put us here."

My heart felt like a lump of lead, its heaviness bursting through my chest. I sat down in one of their little chairs. They were depending on me to be a mother figure. I can't leave them, I thought. If I do, I'll remind them of whomever it was left them alone and caused them to be placed in my care in the first place. How can I, a bride of Christ, also abandon them? But I knew that the Social Service department was busy trying to find good foster homes for them. They would have to get used to someone new eventually.

"You won't be by yourselves. It's not the same," I said.

Trevor was pulling on my cord. The others were sitting on the rug, wide-eyed, wondering what I would say next. I hoped God would give me the ability to say something to help myself and ease the pain I saw in their eyes.

"You see, boys, I'm not going to leave you alone. I'll make sure there's another Sister to take care of you before I go. I'll invite her to come early. I'll see that she knows everyone's name and…and we'll have a party together—all of us!"

I looked around and found only blank stares. Some had turned away from me. Now what? "And…I'd love it if you'd make cards for me. I'm a little bit scared going to this new place. When I look at your cards in the new place, I won't feel so lonely." My eyes were beginning to fill up.

Trevor went to the shelf, took crayons, pencils and construction paper and handed them round. I couldn't believe my eyes.

I managed to put a party together that evening. I was able to get ice cream, cookies, and soda from the kitchen. Sally, Mag's replacement, made Italian pastries. The boys loved the pastries and were jumping around and hugging Sally.

"You gonna take care of us when Sister Maura goes away?"

"No. I have those big boys upstairs to mind. Sister Teresa is coming to take care of you. I'll come downstairs and visit, though," Sally said.

I was glad they liked Sally and knew she'd be nearby. Her warm personality and love of cooking often resulted in parties where our two groups got together, giving brothers who hadn't seen each other since their once-a-month visiting day an added chance to play together.

When Sister Teresa showed up at the party to meet her new charges, the mood changed. They backed away from her the moment she came in the door.

"You fat. And you ain't pretty like Sister Maura. Why you got fat glasses?"

I tried to tell them to be nice and show their good manners, while at the same time, trying to whisper to Teresa that they resented my leaving. I told her not to take their insults personally, but I could tell she was not at all sure she wanted to be there. She tried to be congenial, answering that the fat glasses helped her to see who the good boys were. She talked and worked with individuals, helping them finish the cards they were not sure they wanted to give me now that I was replacing myself with "Sister Teresa of the fat glasses." Some of their illustrations showed a boy sitting or standing alone. The one I tried not to let Teresa see was of a woman in a black witch hat and big sunglasses.

Unable to hide my tears as I hugged each one goodbye, I told myself that this was one of the trials that would improve my spiritual development. I should not be attached to any person, any place, or any thing. That was the rule. Still, I cried myself to sleep worrying that Sister Teresa was not going to appreciate or love them as I did.

Although ethnically mixed in some grades, Holy Family School in Union City had a large population of newly arrived Cubans. Most were non-English speaking. Many of their parents were professionals in Cuba—lawyers, doctors, and teachers—but now, here in America, they had to work as laborers, dressmakers, and housekeepers.

My thirty first-graders were bright and all ready for "big school." In cases of new arrivals from Cuba, I put to use some of the skills on second-language learning that I had developed during my five years as a group mother. My favorite strategy was peer teaching. I found that when children worked and played together, they felt less inhibited trying out new words, and the peer teachers looked on the task as a game, so everyone was happy.

The parents of Holy Family were supportive of my creativity. I planned ceremonies, inviting parents and other family members to celebrate birthdays with a prayer service where the children, who were the guests of honor, would read from original creations of their own.

"Sister Maura," a parent once said, "it's so inspiring that you have the children celebrate their birthdays this way. You must have had a wonderful childhood with celebrations when you were their age."

I didn't tell them that my mother didn't believe in celebrating yearly reminders of "a new mouth to feed every nine months." She used to say, "Birthdays are for them that can afford them."

Observing parents who adored their children, I began to mourn the loss of childbearing. I was twenty-nine at the time, and I knew this was one of the more severe tests I would have to experience. I thought about it sometimes when trying to sleep, but I vowed over and over to fight the loss I felt, refusing to let this mourning interfere with my work.

Directing stage performances gave me the opportunity to dance again, albeit only while I taught. During rehearsals, when the students were comfortable with the steps, I'd dance along with them as though I were one of them, losing myself in the music.

Organizing an international folk dance festival involved visiting the home of an old German parishioner and convincing him to teach me a folk dance from his part of the world. The itinerant speech teacher Beatrice Friedman taught my group a Jewish circle dance. Mexican and Cuban dances were plentiful, and when I added all this to the Fairy Reel and the Walls of Limerick, it made for a colorful production. I felt proud that the tables of international cuisine that filled the school cafeteria were the talk of the school and parish for weeks. We even got a photo in the *Hudson Dispatch*.

In the early seventies, in response to Vatican II's attempt to involve families in the liturgy, home Masses were becoming popular with some American Catholics. But I had another connection. Mass in the home was a reminder of my childhood in Ireland, where such Masses were left over from the time of the Penal Laws, when Catholics had to practice their religion in secret. They provided an occasion to clean, paint, and invite the neighbors to the house for a spiritual celebration. Although the home Masses of the seventies were more of a symbol of independence, allowing the family an opportunity to play a larger role in their spiritual development, I enjoyed the creativity involved. Helping families decide what music to use, write their own prayers, and choose readings helped me feel I was doing what I was meant to do. Still, it was also an uncomfortable reminder of family bonding. When I allowed myself to dwell on the family unit, I knew I was mourning the child I would never have.

Bridie had just given birth to my niece, Caroline. She sent me a picture of her beautiful baby, dressed in pink. I began then to fantasize about having a little girl. I saw her clearly whenever I wanted. She was about four years old and wore a beautiful, rainbow-colored, soft silk dress. Her auburn hair, long and flowing, was tied back, bound with a rose. On her feet were ghillies, ready for Irish dancing. She stood on a stage and smiled at me, though I could never get closer to her than the front row of a huge concert hall. She came and went in my mind. I didn't want to think about her, but whenever she appeared, I let her stay. Sometimes she'd dance for me, light and airy like a princess of the *sidhe*. At other times, she stood on the stage, took a bow, and flew off like a butterfly, changing the colors in her hair and dress to delight me.

Watching parents come to pick up their children after school, I became jealous of the mothers. I found myself infatuated with some of the good-looking fathers and became concerned when I would fantasize about changing places with one of the wives, sleeping with her husband and waking up to take over her role as mother of their beautiful child.

Sometimes I'd feel sorry for myself, thinking this life was unfair to me. Why does God expect me to teach these children, be part of a church family, but not have a child of my own? I wondered later why I didn't share this pain with the Sisters in the house—a bright, modern group of women who were experimenting with the freedoms of Vatican II. In spite of the fact that we all prayed together and shared in cooking and taking care of the convent, I did not feel close to any of them, and I did not feel then I could share my sense of loss. At times, I thought I was the only one experiencing such needs. At other times, I decided that probably they all felt this way. It was something we just had to put up with—one of the trials of religious life. ☙

CHAPTER 24

THE REBELS

I DECIDED TO APPLY TO JOIN the community's first experimental convent—a group of Sisters who lived and worked together without a Mother Superior. They were looked upon as rebels by some of the more conservative members.

"They're taking things too far," if not spoken by well-disciplined tongues, could be seen in doubtful eyes. But I was learning to regain my independence. My opinion as a teacher was respected. I wanted to go forward.

My interview took place in the living room of this convent made up of women mostly under forty. The comfortable chairs and couch too big for the space gave the room a slipshod yet comfortable look. A small television sat in one corner, a record player opposite. The room overlooked a street, where lights from the bodega across the road would make the floor lamp near the bookcase unnecessary if the shade wasn't drawn.

"The interview is just a formality," I was assured by Sister Jenny. "We just need to know that you'll be comfortable with our philosophy."

Each Sister in turn gave her view on what she felt about living and working with the team as a modern religious community.

186 · Maura Mulligan

"It means taking responsibility for our own lives, not asking anyone's permission anymore," Sister Eileen said.

"The main objective being to work with members of the parish community and help ourselves mature as individuals," added Sister Mary.

We talked about the upkeep of the house. Sister Maureen, for example, who seemed to have a talent for bookkeeping, was elected to take care of the finances. And, because of her good organizational skills, Sister Celene was chosen as principal of the school.

"I'm the only one who would take it," she laughed.

"We take turns with cooking," Sister Margaret added. "You don't have to be a good cook. We learn as we go."

When the meeting was over and everyone went to work on school plans, prepare for the next day's dinner menu or discuss the latest scores at Wimbledon, I sat with Sister Agusta and talked. I felt at ease with her. We soon became fast friends.

"Isn't life different since Vatican II? Nothing is as it used to be. We can even stop ignoring the opposite sex," she smiled warmly.

"Well, it's a relief anyway not to have to find a third person to be in the room with you when you're talking to a man." I was referring to the archaic rule that Mother Mistress had tried to implant in our minds: "You are never to find yourself alone with a man—any man—even a relative or a priest."

"It's unnatural how we squelched the desire to socialize with men for so many years."

She stopped talking then because Tina, a young nun, came bouncing into the room. Tina was wearing a pair of jeans, an orange T-shirt and sneakers. She had a guitar slung over her shoulder.

"Sorry I wasn't here for the interview. How'd it go?

"Good. I'm in," I said responding to her hug and welcome. Tina hurried off, saying something about having to prepare songs for the Folk Mass.

"You know," Agusta continued, looking after Tina as she bounced away, "it's not always possible to keep the male–female relationships on a platonic level." She lowered her voice. "Tina's in love with Ron, the assistant pastor."

"Does…everyone know? I mean, is it talked about?"

"Not yet. But it'll come up sooner or later."

But it didn't come up for quite some time. Everyone in the house seemed to be ignoring this new convent phenomenon, as if it were something that was a usual event, like spring following winter. I overheard a conversation one day in the back of the chapel after Ron had celebrated Mass with us. I noticed Tina watching him all throughout the ceremony. She seemed unaware of anyone but him.

"Do you think they'll officially announce it?"

"I'm sure they will. They're good people."

"What if it's all just rumors created by some disgruntled parishioner?"

"No. I saw the way she looked at him during Mass."

I thought a lot about Tina and Ron. I imagined them being romantic together and surprised myself by how genuinely happy I felt for them.

It was Christmas morning when Ron stood up before the congregation to make the announcement that he was leaving the priesthood. He told the shocked parishioners that he had fallen in love and did not want to continue living a lie. There were gasps, but a few people who knew him well applauded his courage.

"You'll get used to it," Ron told the shocked congregants. "We cannot be truly spiritual if we are not true to ourselves."

That evening, Tina told us she was leaving the convent to be with Ron.

This, I think, was the beginning of my own realization that I had serious doubts about the value of living the religious life. I saw how Tina and Ron looked at each other and wished I had a man who would love me unconditionally. Still, I continued to tell myself it was normal to have doubts, especially in the seventies, when so many were leaving religious communities. So, once again, I made myself believe that it was a test from God. I continued to pray for perseverance.

I was doing well in my student-teacher courses at Jersey City State. I even made the Dean's List.

"Not bad for someone who never set foot in a high school," said Agusta, who was becoming, I thought, a good friend.

I laughed, remembering my novitiate days with my tutor, the sleeping Sister Mary Andrew. It was good to finally have a degree like everyone else. Agusta and I saved our allowances and went to the ballet at Lincoln Center. It was great to be in the company of someone else who liked dance. But then, Agusta started to distance herself. She was no longer interested in the ballet or just chatting even. She was studying for a masters degree in science and became engrossed in the geology class she was taking at St. Peter's in Jersey City. Sometimes her work took the form of weekends away studying archeological sites. When she talked to me, it was about her professor, her class, and her homework.

"There's lots of homework," she said one day. "It's important that I please Matt."

"Who's that?"

"My wonderful, handsome professor," she beamed while batting her eyelashes with an exaggerated flourish.

"Oh," I said, feeling like a schoolgirl who lost her best pal. Agusta turned back to her papers and diagrams.

One day, I decided I had to try to talk to her, tell her about my doubts about the religious life. I went to her room and found her pouring over geology papers and books about rock formations.

"Agusta, I need to talk. Is this a good time?"

"No time is good these days," she said. "But Maura, I have to tell you something. You can't tell anyone. Promise?"

"Promise." I was happy we were talking like best friends again. She put down the folder she was holding and sat on her bed.

"I'm in love with Matt. I'm going to leave—to be with him. But Maura, you can't tell anyone. It's so exciting. Only...there's one problem."

"You need a maid of honor." I was joking, not taking her seriously. "I'll be your maid of honor."

"Maura," she sighed, stretching out my name as she stood and threw her hands up. "I'm not getting married. I just want to be with him."

I jumped backwards. She was serious.

"I'm going to make a clean break from the community and— don't take this personally, but I can't be friends with anyone here… including you. Oh, don't look sad."

She sat down, pushing her short black curls out of her eyes. She had been spending her allowance in the beauty parlor.

"It's just that…I've grown away from this life. Sometimes things happen like that. Matt thinks it best that I not maintain old friendships after I leave."

She looked down at her hands, examining her nails.

"Matt thinks? What do you think, Agusta? Don't you think it strange to give up everyone you know just for this guy?"

I was furious. I thought she was being stupid.

"Don't feel bad," she said again.

"Don't feel bad? My best friend is going off with some stranger who doesn't want her to have her own friends anymore, and I'm supposed to be okay with that? I don't see why we can't still be friends. This man sounds like a dictator. Why should he decide for you? We've been friends since I came here."

Then my eyes filled up.

"I'm staying until the end of the year. We'll go to a show or something soon."

She turned back to the folder with "Dr. Matt Jones" written on it in bold red print.

Now who would I tell about my doubts? ᕽ

CHAPTER 25

The Double Loss

*I*T WAS FEBRUARY 25, 1975. Celene was standing at my classroom door, her face tense and drawn.

"I have a…a message for you, Maura."

"I'll be right there," I said wondering why she looked so upset. I'm the one who should be worried, I thought. I lost my friend, Agusta.

I wanted to finish pouring paint into a container for the four students who were about to paint a refrigerator box that the father of one of my students had delivered that day. He cut one side out so it could become a reading corner after it was painted.

My thirty first-grade students were working in small groups or in pairs. Twelve were at the listening center stifling giggles as "The Emperor's New Clothes" reached their ears through the headphones. Three groups of two attached clothespins with words printed on them to words on a wheel that made up compound words. Others were reading to each other in reading corners made out of huge boxes like the one about to be painted.

"There," I said. "They're all settled. You look upset, Celene. What's wrong?"

"I have bad news, Maura. There was a call in the office for you—from your sister. I'm sorry to be the one to tell you this.

Your father died today. I'm so sorry."

"Died? No! There must be some mistake."

Celene touched my arm and said again that she was sorry.

"Someone will take your class. You go ahead over to the convent and call the airlines. Call your sister, whatever you have to do. Don't worry about your class."

"But there must be some mistake. He's not sick. He's not old."

"Go over to the convent. Call your sister."

In a daze I left my classroom, opened the convent door, and headed for the phone room. Petrified, I stared at the two wicker chairs on either side of the phone. I waited for several minutes before I picked up the receiver and dialed. Mag was as calm as the water lilies of the Monet print on the beige wall opposite the chair in which I sat. She had already made airline reservations and booked a car at Shannon.

"You can't be upset. We have to be strong for Mother," she said as we greeted each other at the airport.

"I can't believe it. Is Dad really dead?"

"Bridie called. He had a heart attack. He was cycling to Kilkelly for the groceries and fell off the bike. He died right away. We have to be strong and show Mother it's not the end of the world."

After she said this, Mag looked away. Then she turned and faced me.

"Oh, you. You were always his favorite. You could do nothing wrong."

"Aren't you sad that Dad died? He's only sixty-two!"

"Not really. I'm not sad," she said without hesitation. Then I remembered.

When Mag and I were children, we would fight in bed, kicking each other and making a racket. Dad would come to our bed and wallop Mag with the rod he took from the mantelpiece. I would lay very quiet, and he wouldn't touch me. Mag always got beaten for our noisy bedtimes. She would be beaten again when she wet the bed. I made fun of Mag. She called me a dirty witch, and I called her Pissy Bed.

"I'm sorry he was mean to you, Mag." We hugged and I sobbed

again. I cried on and off for most of the six-hour flight. Mag talked about the idea of Mam moving to England to live with Bridie.

"It would be better for her than being alone."

"Why would it be better? She'll need time to get over her loss."

"We're going to have to be practical about this. We'll stay there for a few days and sell the cattle for her and get her moved out."

"What? We? Why in the world would *we* want to do that? I'm doing nothing of the sort. Mam should decide what she wants to do herself, but she should not do anything for some time. You must be in a state of shock to think of such a thing."

"I've given it a lot of thought." She stood up. "You could never do anything wrong. That's why you have no common sense." She dashed for the bathroom and didn't return to her seat for a long time. I closed my eyes and tried to block out the feelings of aloneness. I was a member of a religious order, and as such, had no say in "the ways of the world." But this was my own home, the part of Ireland that belonged to me. This was my family. But...I had given all that up. I had given up the world. I was miserable, and my bride of Christ status now felt like a prison sentence.

We picked up the car at Shannon and stopped in Galway for lunch. I wished there were someone to cry with, wished Mag felt the way I did. I wanted to tell her to please not mention selling the land and livestock again ever.

As we approached our house, the sun was going down and it was beginning to rain. Some of the village men who had come to the wake were outside the house, backs to the wall, pipes dangling from mouths, talking in quiet Mayo voices. They became silent as we approached the door. Each in turn shook our hands and said the customary greeting, "I'm sorry for your trouble."

The lid of the coffin was leaning against the wall just outside the open door, as was the custom.

When I saw Dad laid out in his coffin near the window, I couldn't stop sobbing. Neighbors talking in quiet voices, sipping their port wine or tea, became silent. Bridie put her arms around me.

"You were his favorite. That's why you're so sad."

Then she said something about morning sickness and ran for the door. I forgot she was pregnant and that she would be worried because of a miscarriage the year before. Mam came towards me with the teapot in her hand.

"Have a sup a tea, A Ghrá. It'll stand to you after your long journey."

I took the teapot out of her hand, put it on the table and hugged her. She seemed bewildered, not tuned in. She wasn't crying and she didn't hug me back. Mag took the teapot and started pouring second cups for the neighbors who told her how well she looked. As soon as she turned her back, they were whispering to each other.

"How many years was Mag in the nuns?"

"You'd never know she was in the nuns at all."

"She has great style, God bless her."

"She's strong, mind you, not crying like Maura."

Their comments aggravated me. I wanted to tell those women to go home, get out of my sight. Instead I focused on the little pink roses on the teacups Bridie was handing round.

We took Dad to the church. All the cars and bikes followed the hearse at a snail's pace. When the funeral Mass was almost over, P.J. arrived. It had been seven years since I'd seen him. I was startled to see my young brother so bedraggled and old looking. His jacket was open, and his once white shirt had turned the color of wild mushrooms. A button was missing. He came into the bench beside me, and when I reached up to embrace him, I recognized a foul smell. It was the same fume-like odor that rose out of the rag I used for cleaning the bar counter during fair days in Kilkelly so many years before. P.J. stumbled on his way out of the bench, going up to the coffin to say goodbye to Dad when the lid was lifted. Mam stood beside him.

After Mass, the neighbors lined up outside the church door. It was comforting to see the familiar faces I had seen as a young girl in Rogers' post office on pension day or at Mass on Sunday. They shook our hands in turn as we passed them, saying they were sorry for our trouble. I felt warmth and support in the grip of their hands. P.J. said he wanted a drink before carrying the coffin to the hearse, but Mam said, "That the divil may blasht and fire to the drink. It has you old and withered before your time. You'll help your brother and your cousins carry your father's coffin to the graveyard, so you will."

P.J., John, and my two cousins Paddy and Thomas raised Dad's coffin on their shoulders—two in front and two in back, arms entwined around each other's shoulders. I could tell by the look on his face that Cousin Paddy, P.J.'s partner, was feeling more than his share of the weight.

The priest blessed the grave with holy water from a small bottle saying, "In the name of The Father and of The Son and of The Holy Ghost." He took the shovel the gravedigger handed him and thrust it into the earth to scatter the first shovelful of clay on my father's coffin, which was now lowered into the grave. A thrush's song from a bush outside the cemetery gate was a stark contrast to the prayers. But the sound of clay on wood dominated all other sounds, the earth announcing its role in the cycle of life.

"Remember, man, thou art but dust, and into dust thou shalt return" were the priest's final words. After his third shovelful of clay, the priest handed the shovel back to the gravedigger.

I allowed my mind to travel back to the Well Field when I was five or six. I was on top of a haystack, and Dad was throwing the soft hay up to me with a pitchfork.

"Tramp it down well. Good girl, yourself."

I felt very important so high up in the air in the middle of the field. If it weren't for me, he said, the hay would never be saved. As the last shovelfuls of clay fell softly on top of each other, I put my arm around my mother's shoulder, wishing she would grab hold of me. She kept looking at the grave. She was motionless.

There was someone standing by the cemetery gate. He was leaning against the pillar and looking towards us. When I looked again, he turned his head, as if not wishing to be recognized. Then I noticed his profile and breathed an audible sigh. I covered my mouth for fear I would cry out loud again. It was my brother

Tommie. He looked as if he were not sure he wanted to approach. I beckoned him to come, and he started walking towards the gravesite, staggering and even more disheveled than P.J. His shoes were untied and his suit wrinkled and stained. He stood behind Mam. She moaned a low, deep groan when she saw him.

"The Lord God Almighty and His Blessed Mother save us! Isn't it hard the life some mothers have?" she said.

When the burial was over, Tommie and P.J. in their drunken daze joined us back at the house. Mag started right away talking about selling the property, contacting the Land Commission and advising Mam to move to London and live with Bridie.

"It's too soon," I said.

"Mother, what do you think of moving in with Bridie? It would be the best thing for you. I'll stay here and help you get rid of the cattle," Mag said ignoring my remark.

"Ah sure I don't know. I don't know."

"It's too soon to make any decisions. Leave her alone," I tried again.

"You don't know what you're talking about. You're too sentimental about the old place. It's no good to her now, and she can't possibly do farm work on her own."

"Why are we talking as if she's not even here?"

"That the divil may set fire to the oul place. It never brought me a day's luck."

"See, she wants to get out of here," Mag said.

I don't remember if anyone else said anything for or against Mam moving to London and the farm being closed up. P.J. and Tommie were searching the house for more booze. Mag was doing all the talking and planning. The following morning, I left to return to the convent. I felt there was nothing I could do or say to change things now. Everyone but me seemed settled with the idea of closing up the house and moving Mam to London. I felt a tearing in my heart and asked Mam to say something about what she wanted, but she had nothing to say.

On the plane to Newark, I cried not only for the loss of my

father but also for the loss of a place in Mayo, Ireland that was once called The Mulligans'. Mam did move to London. She stayed with Bridie for a while and later moved to a senior residence called Nazareth Home.

Mag and I never came to terms with the selling of our land and the closing up of the house. I always thought it was wrong, but she insisted it was for the best. Still, I was happy for her when she fell in love with Don Sullivan. They were married on Samhain Eve three years later. ᔊ

CHAPTER 26

THERAPY SESSION

I NEEDED TO TALK TO A THERAPIST. By the time I decided to call one, I already felt sure I wanted to leave the convent. I was not following Mag. She was sent home. I was leaving of my own free will. I would work with the therapist and then speak to the Provincial Superior, I decided.

In some ways, Vatican II was modernizing the church, but its stand on birth control was archaic. Women could never be decision-makers, even in regards to their own bodies. Nuns were still considered inferior to priests, and women, religious or lay, could not participate as priests. When the statement was issued that the priesthood was not open to women simply because they were not male, it made me stop and think. I recalled how, along with Sister Malachy, I had been a servant to the priest—cleaning his house and cooking his meals. Sister Malachy must have been astutely aware of our status when she suggested that we have a right to play his records. This new awakening had a lot to do with the reason that I joined a picket line in front of St. Patrick's Cathedral in New York. Was I a rebel? All I knew was that I felt I was doing the right thing. I was taking a stand for women's rights. Some people carried signs that read, "Ordain Women Or Stop Baptizing Them." I didn't want to be a priest, but there were others who did. It seemed ridiculous that they were blocked because of their sex. Why should I serve an organization in which women were treated as second-class citizens?

Since therapy was being paid for by the community, I thought it a good idea to learn whatever it was that counseling had to offer me before going out into the world again. Father Jim, the psychologist you saw if you were considering leaving, welcomed me to his office. His blue eyes looked at me with a penetrating yet kind and gentle look.

"So, Maura, what brings you here?"

"I heard it was a good idea to get in touch with my feelings," I said flippantly.

He smiled a knowing smile. He can tell I'm nervous, I thought as he eyed my tightly clenched hands on my lap. No longer in the so-called modern habit, I wore a black knee-length skirt and cream-colored blouse. I wondered if my auburn wavy hair, now cut in the shag style of the day, looked un-nun-like enough to give him the clue that I was thinking of leaving.

I took a slow breath, folded my arms and looked out the window. I didn't know how to begin. Outside, the leaves of the tall tree moving in the evening breeze showed two tones of green. A sparrow flew from its perch on a branch and landed on the windowsill. It seemed to look in at me, turning its head from side to side, as if to say, "Get on with it."

"I'm thinking of leaving religious life, and I want to make sure I'm doing the right thing," I blurted out.

"Okay" was all he said. Not changing his expression, he presented me with a piece of paper and a pencil.

"I always ask new clients to draw a self-portrait on the first visit, Maura. It helps to get things started."

"I can't draw!" I said, feeling panic-stricken.

His look was one of genuine concern when he spoke.

"I'm not looking for a prize-winning portrait, just whatever comes to mind."

"Well, I feel ridiculous. I can't draw," I said, attempting to hand back the paper.

He pretended not to see it, his expression growing slightly more serious, indicating he understood my discomfort. He folded his hands comfortably on his lap and looked at the blank paper. He seemed so practiced and at peace with waiting that I thought he'd wait all night if that was how long it took me to start. I looked again at the window. The sparrow had flown away. How strange that I felt it had deserted me.

"I haven't done any drawing since I was a small girl."

"Like I said, Maura, it's just a way to get us started."

I reluctantly began to draw a girl. I wanted to make her look like an adult, but she came out the way I would have drawn her if I were twelve. When she was finished, she had no breasts, but somehow I had given her a pair of high-heeled shoes.

Father Jim and I were sitting face to face, about three or four feet apart. I wished he would look at his calendar, make a phone call or anything other than sit there and watch me try to draw.

"That's the best I can do on short notice," I laughed nervously.

He reached his hand out to take my high-heeled showpiece, but I held it away, folded it quickly and put it in my bag.

"You still think of yourself as a child, Maura."

"No, I don't think of myself as a child. I just can't draw."

"Tell me about when you were the age of the girl in the drawing."

"I'm annoyed that you said I think of myself as a child."

"I'm glad you're expressing your annoyance. Why does my saying that annoy you?"

"You don't believe that I simply can't draw. And, if you don't believe me, how can I expect you to help me?"

"Well, it's not that I don't believe you. I'm not perfect, but I'll do the best I can to help."

He's trying to be nice, I thought. I may as well be cooperative.

"What should I talk about?"

"Talk about whatever you remember from your childhood. Anything that comes to mind, your earliest memory," he said, nodding for me to start. The look on his face was patient and encouraging.

"My earliest memory?"

Suddenly, although the temperature in his office was comfortable, I felt cold.

"There was a big blizzard when I was six," I began. "It was called 'The Big Snow.'"

"What do you remember?"

"Well, I remember being cold," I said. I wasn't sure if I should go on describing the scene of a long-ago morning when I woke up to find that there was no space between the three stone steps leading from the front door to the field in front of our house. It was a white world. Countless flakes danced between each other, filling the area between the gray sky and fields that were no longer green. The oak tree, my tree, the one I climbed in the spring, loomed over the gable wall and looked to my six-year-old eyes like a huge ghost with too many arms. Surely, there's no point in telling this to a therapist, I thought.

Father Jim smiled. "You were saying you were cold. Did something come to mind? Share any memory at all."

Although I didn't go into detail, I told him about the view in my mind's eye, about the gooseberry and currant bushes that looked like little white hills in the garden. The holy mountain, Croagh Patrick, no longer visible in the distance, hid itself from gathering winds that rattled the windows and doors, whistled down the chimney and swiped wisps of thatch from the roof.

I closed my eyes and took a deep breath. I could see my mother looking at my father when he put the *Farmers' Almanac* back on the mantle behind the bag of tea.

"This flamin' snow will torment us for some time to come, and we won't have a tail to wag with the shoveling that'll be in it."

"Did something come to mind, Maura?"

"Just my family. I remember my parents and my two younger sisters, Mag, five, and Bridie, four. The three of us screamed and jumped up and down, wanting to go outside."

I stopped again, wondering why in the world I was telling this to a stranger. Father Jim put on his waiting look. His eyes were gently inviting me to go ahead.

"Is this what I should be talking about? I mean, how will my telling you stories about my childhood help me?"

"All memories are important, Maura. Did you go out to play in the snow?"

"Yes, and my mother complained. I remember what she said." I thought that I shouldn't use my mother's words because maybe this second- or third-generation Irishman wouldn't understand. But her voice came rushing out before I had a chance to edit it.

"Ye can go out for a small whileen, but let ye not be tormentin' me with trampin' wet snow through the house. I'm fed up to the two eyes with this miserable life."

"What did she mean by a miserable life?"

"She was always saying how motherhood was such drudgery. Anyway, I remember that we pulled on our Wellingtons over our socks and went off to play in the snow," I quickly said. I didn't want to go into all my mother's complaints about her role in life.

"So, anyway," I continued, "those thick, hand-knitted socks squeezed my toes and gave me chilblains. They were just the right size to hang by the fireplace on Christmas Eve." I didn't tell him about the excitement of finding an orange, a few sweets and maybe a small toy in my sock on Christmas morning.

"My mother said we were to wear our old coats in the snow, not our Sunday ones." I laughed, remembering the pixies.

"And what are pixies?" Father Jim wanted to know. His warm smile made me feel for a moment that we were just two people engaged in a friendly conversation.

"The pixies were woolen hats that made us look like elves. They tied under our chins and kept our ears warm."

Father Jim laughed, and I had the uncomfortable feeling that I was entertaining him.

"Are you sure I'm supposed to keep talking about silly memories like snow? Is this what everyone does? I mean, do people come in here, sit down, and tell stories? I just saw someone crying as she left your office," I said, remembering the tall nun he hugged warmly on her way out.

"Getting in touch with your feelings isn't easy. But whatever comes to your mind is what you should bring up. The snow came to the fore, and so it's right to talk about it now. What else do you recall?"

"The snow continued to fall all night, and the path Dad shoveled from the back door to the cow house disappeared by morning. Since the cow house also served as an outhouse, I remember I was glad when Dad shoveled it again. The chamber pot under the bed was getting too full to move."

"No indoor plumbing?"

"No small farms had plumbing back then."

I wanted to say, "Don't you know anything about farm life in Ireland? What kind of an Irish American are you if you don't know what life was like where your people came from?" But I forced my mind to return to the story.

"Well, after a few days, the snow was so deep we could no longer go out to play. Dad shoveled another path to the main road. It led to the town, church or anywhere you wanted to go."

I stopped talking again. I had no words to describe the sensation that the memory of trudging along one of Dad's shoveled paths to the cow house or the road had brought to mind. I had the feeling of being closed in, surrounded by a cold wall on either side. There was nothing to see except white.

"Did something else come to mind," he nudged.

I told him about my oak tree. It felt strange to remember how it no longer felt like a friend when it reached out to gather as many flakes as its ghostly arms could hold. Johnny, who lived in the haunted house beyond the Well Field, said that the snow was as high as the horse's belly. I recalled how we watched Tom Murphy take his horse to Kilkelly to get provisions for people in the village.

I shivered remembering the chill that seeped in through my socks and Wellingtons. My toes were sore when the cold wore off as I sat too close to the fire, my steaming socks dangling over the hot coals. I laughed nervously, wondering if I would ever get used to this, be able to trust Father Jim. As I waited for something else to come to mind, my mother spoke in my head.

"I'm sick and fed up to the two eyes telling you not to put your little feet so close to the fire. The Lord between us, and harm, a síóg like yourself could fall in headfirst. And isn't it in fine fettle we'd be without a way to the doctor. Is it having your father dig his way two miles into Kilkelly for the doctor you'd be?"

"My mother didn't want me to sit too close to the fire," I said. He nodded but said nothing. There was silence again.

"I moved back from the fire because I didn't want to hear her reminding me how I had fallen into the fire when I was three, and how I had put the heart crossways in her with all the bandages she had to prepare, and how I had planned this feat to give her a nervous breakdown."

"Did she have a nervous breakdown?"

"She did, after giving birth to my sister Bridie."

I remembered when Mam would feel bad after shouting at us, how she'd reach for the tin of cocoa over the fireplace. Then, she'd get the blue and white jug of milk and matching sugar bowl from the dresser. We'd drink the hot cocoa and look out at the snow.

"You have happy memories as well as sad ones," he smiled. "We'll explore all of them, and then you'll have a better understanding of yourself."

I felt exposed. I wasn't sure I wanted to go ahead with this business of getting in touch with my feelings. Still, it seemed everyone was doing it, and I wanted to be "with it."

When he urged me to keep going, I shared how the heavy topcoats we used as blankets on the beds felt damp in spite of the airing Mam gave them on the backs of two chairs in front of the fire, and how the coats stayed warm while the steam rose up from their thick collars and sleeves.

"Anything else come to mind?"

"No," I said. But I was thinking how comfortable the smell of Plug tobacco was when it reached out from the pockets of my father's cóta mór. It mingled with the pungent, warm steam from the other coats and the warm bodies of my two sisters who shared the bed with me.

"I remembered wanting to hear the lark," I said finally. "It used to rise up from the hawthorn bush behind the reek of turf."

Father Jim started writing notes on a big yellow pad that waited next to a folder labeled "Maura Mulligan." The sudden movement of his pencil on paper prompted me to look away, to look out the window. Distracted by the pad and the thought that my words were being written down, my eyes returned to the sparrow who was back again, giving witness to my discomfort.

"Go ahead, Maura, what else do you remember?"

"That sparrow out there reminded me of my grandfather. He taught us how to make a bird snare with hairs from the cow's tail, so we could catch a green or gold finch in the snow. We'd put the bird in a cage and feed it until spring came. When it was time to set it free, I was too attached and didn't want to part with it."

The sparrow flew off again.

"That bird there is glad to be free," I laughed, watching it fly away.

"And what does freedom make you think of?"

"I wasn't finished telling you about the snow," I blurted. Suddenly, he maintained his practiced calm look. I knew that he knew I wasn't ready to talk about what being free meant.

"Did your mother and father hug and kiss you," he asked while putting the pencil on the table beside him but keeping the pad on his lap.

"You must be joking. My mother always complained there were too many of us."

"Was she ever affectionate?"

"I remember that she was warm and cuddly when my father used to come home from England. She would clean the house and pick roses from the garden to put on the kitchen table. I liked how nice everything looked. If I said so, she would cuddle me and call me her little síog."

He looked puzzled.

"It means fairy in Irish. You know, one of those creatures who has magic powers and wings." I thought of asking him if he knew Yeats' poem, "The Stolen Child," but then I remembered the Franciscan community is paying him to help me—not the other way around. He asked questions about my father working in England, about how often he left the family to work there. I explained how Mag and Bridie helped with the turf and with picking the spuds. I also told him how after my father left again to return to his job, my mother usually ended up pregnant and resentful. She was always having nightmares and shouting in her sleep.

He started writing in his pad again. Then he looked at his watch. My time was up. ᗡ

CHAPTER 27

GROUP THERAPY

*A*FTER A FEW PRIVATE SESSIONS, Father Jim suggested I join a therapy group session. I wasn't sure I wanted to do this, but he convinced me that people learn a lot about themselves by the way others react to them. When we introduced ourselves, Father Jim told this group of four priests and five nuns, "I'm going to lead you through a fantasy. Now, close your eyes and just tell yourself that you have no vows. You can go where you want with whomever you want, and money is no object." He explained that fantasizing was a way to get in touch with our feelings, that it would help with exploring who we are and ultimately help us make decisions about leaving or staying in religious life.

The others in the group, all at various stages of "getting in touch with feelings," were also seeing Father Jim privately for counseling.

We sat in a circle. I closed my eyes with the others when directed to do so but was already thinking that this fantasy was something I would not participate in. I saw no value in it. I felt we were playing some trendy game. When I closed my eyes, I decided to focus on the rain tapping on the windowpane behind us. My thoughts wandered to a rainy night long ago, when the sky was starless and the moon was waiting to burst from behind dark clouds. The drops on the kitchen window rolled one into another. The turf fire cast a glow on the chunks of smoked bacon that hung, as if by ghostly threads, from the beamed ceiling of our house. A basket of turf was nestled in the corner, inside the back door. Opposite, inside the front door that lead to the Well Field, a bucket of water stood on the three-legged stool that my father used in the morning and evening for milking the cows.

The vision faded suddenly. Father Jim was asking us to open our eyes.

"Who would like to start us off? Tell us anything at all about your fantasy, whatever you feel comfortable with." When no one responded immediately, he said, "What about you, Maura? Where did you go?"

Startled by the sound of my name, I moved around uncomfortably in my chair. I had not followed his directions and didn't want to share the dreamlike memory that had taken over my mind.

"I didn't go anywhere. Just stayed right here," I tried to joke.

Nervous laughter followed. A thin, tall, young priest said he thought I was being uncooperative. When Father Jim asked how I felt about his having said that, I said, "Priests should stop bossing people around." Father Jim laughed, but then reminded me that we were there to react to each other, find out how others see us and learn to understand our own behavior.

The young priest told his fantasy about an affair with a married woman in his parish. They went to Aruba.

"We swam together and made love on the beach," he said.

"Are there any responses to Joe's fantasy?"

"I can identify with you," Doris said. She was a pretty Latina woman with dark hair and eyes. She, too, was preparing to leave her order. As she proceeded to tell about a fling on a beach in Hawaii with a man who looked like Paul Newman, I was thinking that I surely was missing out on something. On the other hand, I couldn't imagine telling fantasies to a group of strangers. What was I doing there? Others in this group said they fantasized about climbing mountains, snorkeling, or skiing. Everyone except a priest who was battling with his sexual orientation went with a person of the opposite sex.

"I think you're just insecure yet," Paul Newman's girlfriend chirped when I said I didn't have a fantasy to share.

As Father Jim pointed out in my next private session, I wasn't willing to be vulnerable, to allow others to react to me.

"I didn't see how it would be helpful. It seemed a useless activity," I insisted.

"Why do you say that?"

"It just seemed like some sort of game to me."

"You're afraid of losing control."

"Maybe so," I agreed.

"The Irish are champions at blocking out feelings," he said.

I began to feel huge waves of sadness. While I sat there wondering what had made me so mournful, I wanted to be hugged and comforted. Father Jim was silent and still. When I looked up, he was nodding off to sleep.

"Oh my God! You're asleep! Wake up and pay attention!"

He jerked his head, obviously startled. "I'm so sorry, Maura! I must have dozed off." He apologized again, then looked at his watch and wrote the next date on his calendar.

We stood up. When it was time to leave, he reached out his arms with a smile. When I fell into them, and he held me, I cried and cried. Suddenly I found myself kissing his face and his eyes. When I aimed at his mouth, he pulled away and smiled gently, holding me at a distance to assure me everything was okay. I realized then what I was doing and wished a hole would open up in the floor and swallow me.

"Oh, I'm sorry!" I said.

"Don't worry. It's okay. It's been a long time since you had physical contact with anyone, especially a man. It's been a long time since anyone held you. It's natural that you would respond in an affectionate way. Please don't worry about it. It's a healthy response." He gave me a quick hug and said he'd see me next week at the same time.

At the next session, I could hardly wait to see what would happen. I looked forward to being hugged again and promised myself that I wouldn't get carried away kissing his face like last time.

But the following week, as soon as I sat opposite him, I knew there was something different in his demeanor. He looked less secure, less comfortable somehow. He was fiddling with a paper in his hand.

"Maura, it's time for you to think of moving on with your therapy. Sometimes a therapist and a client aren't meant to work together. I'm realizing that's the case with us. I think you'll do better work with someone else. I have a list of therapists here, and I'll be pleased to make an appointment for you with any of them."

As he reached over to hand me the list of names, my breath came in short spurts. The years of self-denial and practice in keeping anger at bay helped me to hold myself stiff. I held one hand with the other to steady myself.

"Why? I'm not going to kiss you again. I was beginning to feel comfortable with you," I said, my voice cracking.

I grabbed a tissue with such intensity that the box went flying under his chair. After I wiped my eyes, he handed me the list of names of other psychologists. I crumpled it up, holding it tightly in a ball. I heard none of his explanations about transference and other psychobabble because I couldn't stop crying. I felt thrown away, punished for being affectionate with him.

Finally, between sobs, I forced myself to smooth out the list and look at the four names of three men and a woman. I focused on the name Dr. Helen Kalvin on the west side of Manhattan. I asked if he knew if she was Catholic, and if not, would she understand what my life was about.

"Dr. Kalvin isn't Catholic, but it doesn't matter. She's a good psychologist. She knows and understands the heart and mind."

We said goodbye with a quick hug and he wished me a happy life. ﷼

CHAPTER 28

A New Doctor

I ARRIVED AT DR. KALVIN'S WAITING ROOM an hour early. Her loud voice and Eastern European accent booming from behind her door startled me. I sat trying to read a magazine. I could hear snatches of her exchange with the unfortunate woman whose session I hadn't planned on being privy to.

"Do you zink if you stay vit him you vill be happy?" A pause. "Yes, vell, there you are. You see. You said it yourself. You know he is not good for you."

She might be deaf, I thought. I would ask her if she was. I didn't want everyone on Manhattan's west side hearing her comments on my life.

A man came into the waiting room. He looked surprised, as if he were not expecting anyone to be there. He smiled. His brown eyes had a strained look at first, but then became warmer as his smile deepened. His jet-black hair was receding. He sat opposite me, thumbing through a magazine, a briefcase beside him on the floor. He's terribly early, I thought. He'll hear everything she says to me. My entire session! Panic began to attack. I wondered if I got the time wrong and he was next, not me.

"Excuse me. What time is your appointment wit Dr. Kalvin? I'm wondering why two people are waiting at the same time."

"My session is not with Dr. Kalvin." He jerked his head backwards, pointing his thumb over his shoulder in the direction of another door I hadn't noticed.

"Dr. Hand shares this waiting room with your doc. Boy, she sure is loud."

He looked at his watch. Then Dr. Hand's door opened and I was alone again. I sighed, relieved this man wasn't going to hear my session.

When Dr. Kalvin's door opened, I held the magazine tightly. My shoulders were hunched close to my ears. I noticed that I was resting on my heels with my toes curled upwards. Relax! I almost said aloud. I did not look at the woman leaving.

"Ms. Mulli-can?" Dr. Kalvin pronounced my name with such flair, raising her voice at the last syllable and giving the "g" a hard "c" sound.

I looked quickly at Dr. Hand's door and almost shushed her. Instead, I nodded. She smiled.

"Von't you please come in?"

Her office was twice the size of Father Jim's. Roses in a silver vase adorned a small marble table next to her chair. She motioned for me to sit in the chair opposite and smiled again as she said, "Please sit down."

Compared to my own five-foot-five stature, she was tall. Her gray hair fell softly around her face but didn't hide her plain gold earrings. She looks German, I thought, or maybe Russian. In her simple, brown woolen sweater and skirt that I judged to be about a size twelve, she resembled Baroness Schraeder in "The Sound of Music." I had been thinking about sizes ever since some members of our community had changed to secular clothing a year or so earlier. I knew that I was a size eight. A gold chain completed her outfit. Her smile was warm, so I began to feel less anxious.

"Vell, vot brings you to me?"

Again, I had the urge to hush her up or tell her to speak softly.

"I could hear some of what you said to the woman who was here before me," I mumbled.

"Oh, my goodness. I tend to speak loudly. I sometimes forget," she said in a much quieter tone and not looking in the least surprised by my remark. She had received the referral from Father Jim and was aware of my decision about leaving religious life, she said.

When she asked why I chose a life away from the world, I said I wasn't exactly sure, that there was no one reason—except that when I entered it, I felt I had a vocation. Now it felt right to move on. Her eyebrows went up and she turned her head to one side— the better to hear my explanation of "vocation," I thought. But she was looking for reasons, not explanations.

"Try to zink of vot other motivation you had for choosing that life."

I told her how I felt angry seeing Nuala's friend so depressed and wearing sunglasses to conceal a black eye.

"Those were your first years in America?"

"Yes!"

"You may have been fearful of marrying such a man?"

"I'm sure I was."

"And vot about your parents? How do you zink they influenced you?"

"My mother always said life was difficult and depressing as a wife and mother," I said. Then I immediately wanted to joke, use one of my mother's funny expressions to stop the memories that were filling my mind.

I could see a small, frightened girl with lice in her hair cowering behind a chair, holding her puppy, Spot, tightly. The little girl's mother was on her knees. She was banging her head against the floor, using scary angry words the child had never heard before—words like "fucking bitch of a life." The little girl wanted her other mother back, the one who took her blackberry picking and showed her how to smell the red roses in the garden in front of the house without touching the thorns. She wanted the mother back who told her stories and sang the song about the kitty and the mouse: "Once there was a little kitty, white as the snow. In the garden she used to frolic, long time ago." The mother banging her head on the floor was like some sort of monster, and the little girl wished she would go away and never come back.

The box of tissues next to my chair was almost empty by the time I finished that first session.

My new shrink started each session. Unlike Father Jim, she did not wait for me to get going, and she didn't ask me to draw a picture or go on a fantasy trip.

"So," she said with a warm encouraging smile. "You feel you vant to make another decision now—a decision that will once again change your life?"

I was relieved the way she got right to the point, but there was something else, something about this woman with a strange accent that made me feel a bond with her. I could not think of what it was.

"Right. That's it. I want to make a decision about my life, not influenced by anyone."

"If you decide to leave religious life, vot do you have to do? Vot plans do you have to make?"

"I have to find a place to live. But, first, I have to meet with Mother Provincial and tell her my decision to leave. Then, because I made final vows already, I have to get a dispensation from The Holy See—from Rome."

"That sounds like a lot of work. Vot vill you tell your Mother Provencal? Vill she ask why?"

"Even if she doesn't ask why, I'll need to tell her why."

"Okay. Vot vill you say?"

"I'll say…I don't know."

She smiled. "You must think about the new life you want for yourself."

When I arrived for the next session, the brown-eyed man was in the waiting room ahead of me. He smiled when I sat down, and I wished he weren't there again. I wanted to go over what I was going to say about what I thought I wanted for myself.

"Hi. Looks like we have the same time again this week?"

I nodded, not really wanting to start a conversation with him.

"I'm Philip."

He smiled warmly, his eyes drawing me into their brownness. Dr. Kalvin opened her door. If she noticed my flushed face, she didn't say anything about it.

"I've been thinking that most of all, I want to feel free," I said when we were in her office.

"Vot vill you do when you are free?"

"I want to have my own space, not have to share with a bunch of other women. I want to walk around a room and know that the whole space is just for me. Maybe I can find a man to love?"

"You're an attractive woman. I have no doubt you will."

That opening led to more tears about my disappointment with Father Jim.

She wanted to know more about my childhood. For the next few sessions, that's all we talked about.

In time, I realized the bond we shared was immigration. She, too, came from somewhere else. I wished then we could just have a conversation instead of a therapy session. I wanted to know about her country of origin and how it was for her coming to America. She also had to get used to another culture and make her way in a new world.

"You came from somewhere else, too?" I ventured.

"Yes, I came from Russia." She pronounced it with an "o" instead of a "u." "But we better not talk about me or ve von't get all your questions answered."

When I thought about what it must have been like to learn a new language and study to become a doctor, I felt braver about exploring my fears of leaving a secure existence and finding new adventures in the world.

A couple of months of therapy later, I left Dr. Kalvin's office with a sigh that was a mixture of pain and relief. My session that day had been the hardest, the most painful session ever. I'd tried to tell a story I had kept locked inside for decades. My sentences were short because it was difficult to breathe.

"My mother had only a few chickens that spring. They must have been like gold. When she saw Spot chasing the chickens, she…"

"Yes, go ahead."

"She took him by the hind legs and…"

"Yes?"

"She bashed his head against a tree."

"Oh my God!"

"He died the next day"

I said it as quickly as I could. I needed to vomit it up and spit it out. I used the entire box of tissues on the table.

"Poor Spot!" I repeated over and over.

I was unable to tell her that I ran to him and clasped his bloody body in my arms and that I took him to the river to wash the blood. Nothing since has ever been so painful to admit as my own mother killing my pet.

"How dreadful! She hurt you more than you could bear, and it was awful for you. She had to be very disturbed to do that."

When I left her office, my eyes still red, I could feel the July heat on the cement through the soles of my slingback sandals. Now that I had told that painful memory, I wondered if I would feel healed. Would I feel forgiveness for my mother and be able to move on? The sun would help dry my tears. While I walked and walked, more memories returned.

Before she killed Spot, Mam used to take me blackberry picking. She carried an old bucket that was fixed by the tinker man who snatched the cock and the drake from the wall outside the henhouse. I had seen him throw a canvas bag over their heads and run away.

"That the divil may fire him outta the country," Mam said. "God blast the thief anyhow, and me after giving the flamer two shillings for slapping an oul piece of tin on the leak in the can."

There were clusters of fine ripe berries in the bushes behind the henhouse, she told me, "but be careful where you step. There might be a clocking hen or two hatching under them. The divil is in some of the hens for going away before them when they're ready to hatch. Between the tinkers, your dog, and the fox, the poor things might as well carry a sign saying 'Take me away.'"

I had to hold Spot while she picked the berries behind the henhouse because she looked at him suspiciously.

"He'll be all right in the Well Field where he can keep himself occupied with rabbits," she added.

When we ran out of ripe berries on our own land, Mam let us take the cans with us on our way to school. We hid them behind the wall near Heneghans' well and retrieved them after school. We picked berries all along the road, and it took us hours to get home. Mam liked having blackberries in the house.

We put some in a bowl with milk and sugar for after tea. The others, Mam put aside for "bottling."

"The bottling is time taking, but 'tis worth it," she told Mary Murphy. "If you take a gallon of the blackberries, a good bit of sugar, and two gallons of lukewarm water, you have the makings of a few good bottles."

"How much sugar?" Mary Murphy wanted to know.

"Oh, the divil is in the amount of sugar it takes. You'd need a pound to the gallon if you want it sweet enough."

To hurry the process of blackberry winemaking, Mam sometimes boiled the blackberries and sugar until they became like jam. She then strained the juice with a mesh cloth and poured the liquid into bottles. After she corked them, she stored the concoction in the press in her bedroom.

A few weeks later, sometimes in the middle of the night, we'd hear corks popping. Everything changed after the corks popped. It was as if my mother became someone else at this time every year, and I could not understand why popping corks in the middle of the night brought about such a change in her.

She spent a lot of time in "the room below" (her bedroom) with the blackberry bottles. She always kept the door closed. Doors were peculiar with her during blackberry season. She forgot to close the henhouse door at night, so the fox came for nightly raids.

Since "the bushy-tailed bastard" stole the hens, she sometimes stayed awake looking out the window, trying to catch him. If she did, she said she'd "brain him with the broom handle."

She watched Spot, too. She looked at him as if he were the fox.

"Spot chases the chickens for fun," I tried to tell her, but she didn't believe me.

One blackberry season, dead, diseased rabbits were everywhere—on the side of the road as we walked to school, inside the school gate, and along the riverbank where we played in the evening. The farmers couldn't dispose of them fast enough, and some said they had to keep the dogs tied up for fear they might catch the disease as well.

I hated to see their swollen heads and the way their eyes were bulging out of their sockets. Mam said the whole world was gone mad.

My father was getting ready to go off to England again. He read out loud from the newspaper that some doctor inoculated two wild rabbits at Maillebois in northern France in an attempt to rid his property of the animal. "The two that got the needle spread the bloody myxomatosis all over Europe."

He paused to relight his pipe. He looked at me where I was crouched by the hearth, my face in my hands. He must have known I was mourning because he stroked my hair and shook his head from side to side took a deep breath. Then he looked at my mother. "Let you stay away from blackberry bushes anyhow," he mumbled.

"And what's it to you? A lot you know or care," she said, thrusting the milk bucket into his chest.

He grabbed it, said nothing, then turned on his heel and went out to milk the cows. When he came back, he stood in the middle of the floor and looked at her, the bucket of warm milk in one hand and the milking stool in the other.

"Making and drinking that bottled stuff is no good for you. You should give the blackberries a rest."

He plopped the bucket of milk on the table like a heavy bag of potatoes.

"And what do you know about anything around here, and you gone away to England half the year," she spat through her teeth. "Why the divil don't you look for work at home, now that the County Council is fixing roads from here all the way to Ballyhaunis? Sign up for road work, why don't you, instead of going away before you to a foreign country?" She grabbed hold of the straining cloth roughly and started to strain the milk.

Dad put on his coat and got on his bike without a word. He came home a couple of hours later and showed the working papers to Mam.

"Thanks and glory be to God," she said. Her eyes lit up, and she started tidying the kitchen. When it was swept and dusted, she picked flowers from the garden and asked me to put them on the table in a jam jar filled with water. Although I was still angry with her, I liked arranging the flowers. It was as if someone were coming to visit.

My father stayed in Ireland that year and the year after, while the East Mayo roads were being repaired. While he stayed home, Mam cooked rashers and eggs for his breakfast. She sang songs like she used to when she expected him home at Christmas: *Red is the rose that in yonder garden grows. Fair are the lilies of the valley. Clear is the water that flows from the Boyne. But my love is fairer than any.*

"Let ye eat the blackberries as ye pick the flamin' things and make jam if ye want. I'm washing my hands of them," she said.

After that, there was no more forgetting to lock the henhouse at night, and she stopped threatening to brain the fox with the broom handle.

Although there was an alteration in her behavior, there was no change in me. I continued having nightmares about Spot. I stopped calling her Mam. I had no name for her. I tried not to address her at all. She looked at me, shaking her head, biting her lower lip. I think maybe she wanted to ask my forgiveness for killing Spot, but all she said was, "God help you, A Grá. You're too sensitive for your own good, and there's a lot you don't understand in this world." She said this over and over again, staring at me with wrinkled forehead and hurt eyes. I looked away.

"I understand plenty!" I screamed silently. I wanted to shout it out loud, but I refused to give her the satisfaction of speaking to her. When I went to Mass on Sunday, I asked God to help me forgive her. God seemed not to be doing his job at all. I still felt the same anger and hate when I came home. I told the priest in confession that I was angry with my mother. He gave me absolution and told me that God forgives me. I thought about telling Dad how I felt, but I didn't know what to say.

Before Mam killed Spot, I had been begging to go to step dancing class. I had brought it up several times, but Mam always said we didn't have the nine pence for the class. Since she stopped making blackberry wine, there was another change. She was actually telling me to *go* to the dancing master.

"Your father is working. We have the nine pence. You'll be a good dancer. You have the build, and the shapely legs that you inherited from me. 'Twill do you good. Go and learn the steps."

I wanted to dance more than anything in the world. I tried to pretend that Spot was still alive so I wouldn't feel so angry, but it didn't work. I wouldn't go to the dance class because *she* was now encouraging it.

I would visit with Marion to escape my mother. Marion had new books she got from her aunt in New York. I borrowed *The Wind in the Willows* and sat on the grass under a tree in the garden, letting myself wander away with Toad and Badger. I forgot about feeling angry for a while.

When Mam stopped telling me to go to the dance class, I asked Marion if she'd come with me. She wasn't keen at all about dancing but said she'd go because we're friends. In the end, Marion was the one that told Mam we had decided to attend the dance class.

Mam looked happy. She took a shilling and a three-penny bit out of her handbag and put it on the kitchen table. "There's six pence extra for ice cream," she said. I pretended not to see it.

She looked at me sideways, picked up her *ciseeán* and went to the henhouse to collect the eggs. That's when I took the money off the table.

Marion and I left our bikes outside the Knock school gate along with all the others. The teacher, Séamus Forde, told us to sit at the desks that were pushed back around the perimeter of the room and wait a while. The regular students stood in straight lines. When Mr. Forde counted to three—*aon, dó, trí*—he put his lips in an "o" shape and started whistling a reel. They all began to dance together at exactly the same time. I thought they looked marvelous and couldn't wait till he called us beginners on the floor.

"We'll never learn that," mumbled Marion. "Come on. Let's go to Byrne's for ice cream before he misses us."

"Sit down, you eegit," I said fiercely while tugging at her sleeve. "Of course we'll learn it. He'll give us easy steps first. Sit down."

Marion reluctantly threw herself on the seat again and put her head on the desk. I watched in awe as the dancers made chains, arches and circles. They moved their feet quickly all at the same time. Even Bernadette O'Malley, who always called Peggy Boyle's sewing "a work of fart," was looking good. I couldn't believe that the two of them were hand in hand, making an arch to let the others pass through in a "thread the needle" movement. I didn't understand how in the world the steppers knew when to stop all together.

Marion was looking at the dancers with only one eye. She had her hand to her head, covering the other side of her face. When it was time for the beginners to go out on the floor, she whispered, "I'll meet you at Byrne's shop," and headed for the door.

"Come back here, Miss," the dancing master laughed. He was not at all like the headmaster at school. He patted Marion on the arm and told her not to worry. When we lined up, Mr. Forde danced the sidestep of the reel very slowly. "Hop, *aon, dó, trí, ceathar, cúig, sé, seacht,*" he counted, taking seven steps across the floor, one foot behind the other. He told us to hop high off the ground. We practiced all together, and I felt as if I were flying. I forgot all my worries and knew that moment that I'd practice until

I was as good as the advanced students.

"What way was the dancing class?" asked Mam when I got home.

"Grand," I said, forgetting I wasn't talking to her. She smiled. I looked away quickly.

"Durkin's bitch has a new litter of pups," she said. "They'll want to be giving them away in a few weeks." She threw a sod of turf in the fire to hurry the dinner. "The myxomatosis won't last forever. The rabbits will become plentiful again in no time, and we'll need a dog to chase them away from the heads of cabbage."

When I shared these childhood memories with my therapist, she said I was beginning to forgive Mam. ∽

CHAPTER 29

PHILIP

*T*HE FOLLOWING WEEK, Philip was waiting outside the building where our therapists worked. He stood on the bottom step, open briefcase in hand, looking at mail. His smile was hesitant as I emerged.

"Hi again. I was just going to grab a bite. Do you have any plans?"

"Plans?"

"I mean, would you like to join me for a bite to eat?"

He tried not to look at my red eyes as he closed his briefcase, switched it to the other knee and then opened it again.

"If you'd rather not, maybe we could do it some other time? I know what it's like to have had a difficult session. I've had my share of them."

I dabbed my eyes with a tissue. The distraction was a relief, but I wasn't sure I wanted to have dinner with a man I had never had a conversation with. Platonic relationships with the opposite sex were lately being encouraged for religious. Of course, those platonic friendships didn't always stay that way. Nonetheless, it was now considered healthy for nuns to go ice skating, play tennis and even go out to dinner with male friends. However, most of these platonic friends were priests or religious brothers who were also inexperienced in relating to the opposite sex. In most cases the others in the convent would have known them through work or parish involvement. That wasn't the case here. Still, I thought, I need a distraction, and I'm getting ready to leave the convent anyway. Maybe it will be a good idea?

"Okay. Sure."

"Oh, great! There's a nice pizza place on Seventy-Fourth and Columbus. We can just walk there. That okay with you?'

"Fine. I wanted to walk anyway."

There was the uncomfortable feeling of not knowing what to say as we walked.

"Where do you live?" Philip asked.

"Live? Me? Oh...I'm in a...New Jersey."

"Really? I have a friend who lives in Weehawken. Where abouts do you live?"

I must have looked confused because he said with a laugh, "It's not a secret or something?"

"What?'

"Where you live. You're not in the secret service or something? Uh-oh! You have a jealous husband!"

"Oh no, nothing like that."

"I'm on Seventy-Eighth, just off Broadway," he said, temporarily relieving me of my discomfort.

"I'm an attorney. And you? What do you do?"

"Oh, I'm a teacher."

"Public school?"

"No. Catholic school."

"Uh-oh. You have to work with nuns?"

I tried to laugh, but I felt annoyed.

"What's wrong with nuns? The ones I work with are very nice."

"Nice? Don't they make kids stand in the corner and beat them with a ruler?"

This wasn't going to be as easy as I thought. Why did I ever agree to a meal with a stranger and his luring eyes? What was wrong with me? Well, I was only walking down the street with him. I could change my mind any minute.

His stereotypical view of nuns bothered me. I had to defend them, even if I was planning on leaving them.

"For your information, nuns these days use modern teaching methods and help kids learn about caring for one another," I said calmly.

"Oh, I didn't mean to offend. Let's change the subject. What do you want to talk about?"

"I don't know. How's your therapy going?" I said.

"Oh, let's not get into that!"

"Well, I'm new at the therapy thing, and I just wondered how long it takes?"

"How long? Guess that depends on the individual. I've been going to my guy longer than I'd care to admit." He looked uncomfortable.

"At least you can't hear him halfway down the block," I said, happy to lighten the situation.

"True. Does what's-her-face know she's as loud as she is?"

"She's really very nice. I've told her she's too loud."

"Well, good for you. Someone should tell her."

There was silence for a while before Philip said, "So, are you married?"

"No. I'm looking for a millionaire husband. Do you know any?" He laughed.

I wondered how I was going to keep this banter going. This may be a nice man. I could have a new friend—maybe down the road, fall in love with him? I should tell him who I am and that I'm considering leaving the convent. No. He has already formed a negative opinion of nuns. He'll reject me before he ever gets to know me.

"Rich men?" he said. "Would you settle for a date with a nice, single guy who thinks you're very pretty? I'm not talking about today, of course. This isn't a date. It's just dinner together to get to know each other. Well?"

"Oh!"

Philip stopped walking and looked at me. What's with this thirty-something woman, he must have been thinking to himself. She's acting like someone from another planet. He tried another question.

"What do you like to do? Any hobbies?"

"Oh, I like to dance. I love to dance. I'm a dancer."

"Are you professional? You sure look like a dancer with that graceful walk of yours," he said as we entered the restaurant.

I smiled broadly, happy to gobble up the compliments and finally have something safe to talk about.

"So, do you perform?'

"Well, I used to perform, when I belonged to a dancing school."

"Why'd you stop?"

"Oh, I just wanted to do something else, I guess. But I think I'm going to go back to dancing again soon."

"Well, if you're performing anywhere, let me know and I'll go. Okay?"

"Okay. I'll be sure to let you know"

After chicken cacciatore and a glass of Chardonnay, we had ice cream and coffee. When Philip asked for my phone number, I panicked again. It didn't occur to me that he would ask for my number. I was just enjoying the novelty of having dinner with a man—a big change from always eating with women. It was rare for me to have the chance to talk about the Irish Dance world. He was interested in my description of the feis, getting a competitor's number, entering the competition for Mayo champion and winning first runner-up before I left Ireland. I told him about winning first prize in the Open Reel in Canada the year after I came to America. Then I became quiet, remembering how I gave up dancing for a whole year before entering the convent, just to see if I could do it. It was a great loss in my life because I cherished going to class, performing, and competing.

"So, can I call you? There's something…. I can see it in your face. You do have a jealous husband, don't you?"

"No, I don't have a jealous husband."

"Well, it's just that you're...Can I call you?"

"My phone is out of order. It should be fixed soon. When I see you in the waiting room next week, I'll give you the number then. Okay?"

"Well, okay, but you sure are mysterious, Ms. Maura."

We said our goodbyes, and I thanked him for dinner by reaching out my hand to shake his. As he shook my hand, he leaned forward and kissed my cheek. His lips were soft and warm, causing me to instinctively put my hand to my face. As we parted, I was glad to not have to think up any more lies.

My therapy session flashed before my mind as I took my seat on the bus. I had a lot to deal with. I would not add a new friendship based on lies to my list. I decided I would tell Philip the truth next week. If he didn't want to be my friend, then it wasn't meant to be.

Philip stopped eating and stared at me as if I were telling some sort of joke.

"That's not even funny. Nuns are old, unattractive, and wear habits. You don't exactly fit the description. Why are you saying this?"

"Well, I've told you. Now I feel better."

I took a roll out of the breadbasket and proceeded to butter it. The relief I felt must have shown in my face because Philip stared at me for several seconds, then he dropped his knife.

"You're serious, aren't you?" he yelled, causing people at the next table to turn and look at us.

"Stop yelling! Yes, I am serious. And you should know that nuns are not ugly, and only a few are mean or old—just like people from any walk of life," I said in a hushed voice.

"Well, oh my God! I should say not...if you're one."

He stared at me for what seemed an age. I just kept eating my roll slowly and feeling very good about being truthful. Finally, he spoke.

"So, what does that mean now? Can we go out or what?"

"Well, I have vows I must keep for now. But we can be friends. We can go to dinner, concerts, movies, anything as friends."

"As friends?"

"We all need friends, Philip."

"Well, I'll be damned—Oh! Excuse me."

"Now don't start changing the way you talk to me. I'm still the same person."

"Oh, no you're not. And if I call you, who will answer the phone?"

I had to smile. His nervousness made me feel closer to him. ༄

CHAPTER 30

THE APARTMENT

WE SAT OPPOSITE EACH OTHER, eye to eye. The days of kneeling while talking to the Mother Superior were gone. Good riddance to them!

"Take a year of exclostration," said the Mother Provincial. "It will allow you to think things through. When the year is up, you'll then decide to return to the convent or leave the community. You'll continue to live your vows for the year, have your own paycheck to take care of your bills, and the community will take care of doctor bills."

"Doctor bills? My sessions with a therapist, too?" I wondered aloud.

"Whatever you need. And if you ever want to talk..." she reached to touched my arm, "I'm here."

I wondered if she hoped I'd change my mind. I felt greatly relieved, visualizing myself living alone in my own space, decorating it myself, being in charge of my own life.

"I appreciate your support," I said.

She smiled wistfully and turned her eyes to the window, where the Hudson River and Bear Mountain were exclaiming the wonders of creation.

"How is your sister Margaret?" she asked suddenly. I jumped. That she had left without any explanation was still haunting me. I knew the community had sent her home because she was sick, but I still didn't know why they would do such a thing. I wish we could have talked about it. What was wrong with her health, anyway?

Instead of asking Mother Provincial, the only other person besides Mag who really knew the secret behind her exit, I said I remembered she wore her habit when she left the Mother House in Peekskill. She changed her clothes at the Kennedy Home (a children's home in the Bronx run by the order) and left from there. I never asked Mag what really happened when she left. I didn't want her to feel shame if she actually was sent home. I was trying to follow the rule of not discussing why someone left.

"Oh, indeed. Many Sisters left without saying goodbye to anyone, because that was the way it was."

When I stood to leave, Mother Provincial embraced me and reassured me that she was there if I needed to talk. I could see she wanted what was best for me, though she must have hoped I'd change my mind. Many were leaving in the seventies, and there were few signing up to take their places.

For the first time in my life, I would soon live in a place all by myself, a space I wouldn't have to share with anyone. My heart raced. It was a powerful feeling of ownership of my own person. Anita, who was also on leave, said she'd help me look for an apartment. Her leave was different because she wasn't actually thinking of leaving the community. She lived away from the convent so as to take care of her sister, who had suffered a mental breakdown.

We looked in *The Jersey Journal* and the *Hudson Dispatch* for an apartment that my measly income would cover. It was a thrill to actually have my own paycheck in hand, although the thought of dealing with money after so many years of rejecting it frightened me terribly. Since my arrival in America, I had never been inside a bank. I was terrified at the thought of actually walking into a bank and opening an account. When I worked for the phone company sixteen years earlier, I cashed my check every two weeks in the company's office, paid Cousin Nuala the room and board, sent a few dollars home to Ireland, and spent the rest on dance classes and clothes. Now, my very first take-home paycheck from St. Ignatius School on the Upper East Side of Manhattan was in my bag. But getting it from there to a bank was like going into Mother Mistress's office for the first time. I was petrified. I thought that the bank employee would think how strange it was that a woman in her late thirties should be opening her first checking account. I worried I wouldn't know what to say after requesting to open an account. I didn't want to ask anyone for help because I couldn't admit how scared I was and how dumb I felt. So much for the novitiate training in humility! I rehearsed a possible conversation with the bank clerk.

"I wish to open an account."

"What kind of account?"

"One where I can deposit my paycheck."

"That would be a checking account, Madam. What other accounts do you have with us?"

This is when I'd stop my rehearsal and make my mind blank. If I worried anymore, I'd never go through with it. Finally, one day, I went to a branch of Chemical Bank, near the school on 84th and Madison. It was a relief that the clerk didn't ask what other accounts I had. Still, I felt she knew I was nervous by the way she looked at me. Dr. Kalvin assured me that there were others out there who were fearful of money, too—women who let their men take care of the finances and then found themselves alone after a divorce or death.

I had other fears—nightmares about men. When I tried to recall the dreams, I thought I heard moans and groans coming from my parents' bed. My child's mind told me my mother was in pain, and although my adult mind told me her moans could have been the result of pleasure, I still remembered the fear of going back to sleep.

It was time to make my mind blank again. Problems sometimes went away when I didn't think about them. Boyfriends waited all these years; they could wait another while. I began to tell myself to think about being free. Getting my own apartment would be a start.

Once I had opened the checking account, I felt I could look for a place. I'd have to pay the deposit with a check. Anita and I set off on foot with a list of addresses of affordable apartments we had found in the local newspapers. The first place we tried had overflowing garbage cans in front of the building. At the next address, a rat greeted us at the front door. We tried a few more with similar results.

"Let's look at buildings not listed in the newspaper," Anita said finally.

"Good idea. Let's pretend I can pay any amount of rent, just for fun. Then we'll look seriously again another day."

We were shown around a few posh new buildings overlooking the Hudson on Boulevard East, and I pretended the view of the Hudson wasn't good enough or that my husband wouldn't approve of this or that detail of a lovely deck. I couldn't believe that the people showing us around were taking me seriously. I wanted to apologize for deceiving them, but Anita talked me out of it, saying they were probably used to hearing comments like that. She asked how I thought up such a thing. "Just practicing for going out into the world," I said.

Finally, we came upon an old, ivy-covered, walk-up building that looked like a castle. The hallways and stairs were swept clean. Blasts of Latin, Caribbean and Indian music were coming from behind closed doors. Good. Multicultural, I thought. My Chieftains and James Galway records will fit right in here. The three-room apartment with an eat-in kitchen in the rear was just right. I'd put up curtains to hide the small courtyard with pigeons fighting for a space on the fire escape. Although the Hudson River was outside the front door with a magnificent New York skyline on the other side, I had to run down four flights of stairs for the view. When I signed the lease, Anita nudged me, pointing to the signature: Sister Maura Mulligan. "Oops," I said. When I crossed out the title I had been living with for sixteen years and looked at my name, the feeling was one of coming home to myself. I needed to stand still for a few minutes and absorb it.

With great excitement, I invited Philip to see my new place. His eyes took in the three rooms at once and his mouth opened when he saw the eat-in kitchen.

"This is fantastic! I'm amazed you could find such a great deal."

"Gee, Philip, thanks for all that faith in me. But I'm glad you approve."

"I'll help you paint and do the floors," he said with enthusiasm.

"Wonderful! I'll have a painting party. I'll invite Mag and Don. They volunteered as well."

"A painting party?" Philip groaned.

"What's wrong with that? Don't you want to meet my sister and brother-in-law?"

"It's not that I don't want to meet them." He stood up and started to pace. I followed him from the living room to the kitchen and back again. I was visualizing a table here and a wall hanging there. I wasn't in the mood for Philip's distress, whatever it was.

"Would a mirror look good on that wall, Philip?"

"Look, I decided to go to AA," Philip said looking at the floor. "I didn't tell you before, and I've always been careful when I'm around you but—well, I'm an alcoholic."

"What?"

"Last time I got drunk, it was at a painting party. I got myself arrested afterwards for indecent exposure."

Philip looked at me, searching my eyes for understanding or pity—neither of which I possessed at that moment. He took a step away when he saw what must have been horror and panic on my face.

"You didn't just say that," I said to the parquet floor.

"Maura, why are you so shocked? You told me about your brother Tommie being an alcoholic. Sometimes people do crazy things when they're drunk."

I walked into the empty kitchen and stared out the window. The two cooing pigeons on the fire escape looked back. I thought of Mag and me wandering around London from pub to pub three summers earlier. Bridie had warned us that Tommie was in bad shape, and that neither she nor P.J. knew where he lived. When we found Tommie in The Rat and Parrot, the only pub he hadn't been thrown out of, we tried to talk to him as if it were a perfectly normal way to visit your brother after having traveled three thousand miles to do so.

"Here you are, Tommie. How are you?"

"Who's this now? Want a drink?"

"It's me, Maura. Mag is here, too. We came from America to see you, Tommie."

"Hello, Tommie. Good to see you," Mag said, reaching out to hug him. I moved closer and joined in the hug. He held us with such force I wanted to cry. I wished I didn't want to pull away from the foul smell. When he let us go after what seemed an eternity, I felt tears pushing their way out. I needed to protect him from the pain in his life. I saw myself standing between him and the blows that life was dealing him, just as I had done when he was a little boy and my mother was beating him. I was able to save him then and make her stop.

In the London pub, I put my arm around him. He wiped his face with the too-long sleeve of his jacket. When he stiffened his back and took a long drink of his pint, I let go of him. He was thin, I thought, and smaller than I had remembered. His clothes seemed to hang on his bony body. There were beer stains and splashes of paint on his pants. His boots were covered with bits of hardened cement.

"Have a drink. What'll ye have?" He was taking coins out of his pocket, putting them on the counter. "Pity ye didn't come a few hours ago."

"Here, let me buy," I shouted in his ear so he could hear me above the loud din.

"I thought you was in the nuns. Did you come out?" He was staring at the green wool pantsuit I wore.

"No. We can wear secular clothes when we're on vacation."

"What?"

"I said we can wear regular clothes when we're on vacation."

"On vacation? You sound like a Yank. Hell, you are a Yank sure." He laughed, showing five brown teeth.

When the barman brought him a pint of Guinness and glasses of ginger ale for Mag and me, we moved further away from the bar. I was coughing because of all the smoke. My throat was beginning to get sore from shouting to be heard. Lads were loud and rough as they pushed and shoved to move past us, trying to get closer to the bar.

I started to move towards the door. Mag held on to Tommie's sleeve, dragging him along, following me.

"Can we see where you live, Tommie? I need to get out of this smoke," I said.

"No. I keep where I live a secret. Here, have another drink," he said nodding towards the barman, staggering in an attempt to move back to the spot he had vacated before we dragged him away.

We awkwardly said goodbye, with him wanting to hug us and draw us back to the counter and us shouting, "We'll see you soon again, Tommie."

On the way back to Bridie's, Mag confided in me that her husband had a problem with drink as well. I remembered then the previous Easter Sunday when I had gone to Don's parents' home for dinner. His brother Jim was out looking for Don, up and down the block of their Brooklyn Street. Don had gone to the store to get more beer. When it started to snow, he couldn't find his way back.

"Well, on holidays and weekends, he puts on a load." Mag had learned some strange expressions since leaving the convent. "He's okay otherwise. He keeps his job and everything."

In the glaring light of the London underground, I saw a look of resignation and disappointment as she turned her beautiful face away from me. That night, I couldn't sleep. I knew Mag was awake in the twin bed alongside mine, but we didn't speak.

"Maura," Philip was saying. "Where are you?"

"It's a horrible disease, Philip," I said without looking at him.

"Tell me about it."

"I don't want to think or talk about it anymore! I picked up the broom and started sweeping the floor, but Tommie's blurred eyes seemed to stare at me from the stained boards.

"Hey, I just swept that floor," Philip said.

I turned away. I had secretly hoped Philip would become my lover. We'd get married, and he'd be the one who would always be there for me. Now, I wasn't sure I even wanted him as a friend. His hunched shoulders, as he moved slowly away from me to sit on the windowsill, made me realize how much he was hurting. I didn't know what to say to make us feel better. Finally, I just wrapped my arms around him. We held each other for a long time.

The following week, I planned the painting party. Don showed up with two six-packs in a brown shopping bag. Mag carried the paintbrushes. Philip had arrived ahead of them. He looked at the beer in Don's hand and watched him put it in the refrigerator.

"We'll have a drink *after* we finish," Don said with a wink to Philip. A bit of small talk followed. We decided to each take a room. I took the bedroom, Mag began working on a wall in the living room. Don stayed in the kitchen so he could be "near the beer." Philip started on the ceilings.

"I'll do the bedroom ceiling first to be near you," he said giving me a teasing hug.

We worked quickly without much talking. When I went to the kitchen for a glass of water, Don was taking another beer out of the refrigerator. There were two empty cans on the floor beside him.

"Come on, Phil. Have a beer! No man should drink alone," he yelled. Don held a bottle of beer out to Philip, who had followed me into the kitchen.

"I'm okay, Don, thanks. Maybe later."

Good, I thought. Philip is strong. He's not going to drink. Mag was doing a terrible job in the living room. The wall she was painting was streaked, and there was paint all over her clothes and hair.

"Mag, take a break. You're going too fast. Have a glass of juice or something."

"The sooner we get finished, the better. I'm not feeling well," she said.

"Then don't paint anymore. Let's go for a walk. Let the men finish."

"No. Don will just keep drinking until the beer is all gone. I wish Philip would help him drink it," she whispered.

I managed to coax her out for a walk. We walked along Boulevard East and went for tea to The Green Kitchen a few blocks away. An hour later, I noticed Mag bracing herself as we climbed the four flights of stairs to the apartment. I could hear the men talking loudly.

"They're drunk," Mag said as I opened the door. They were sitting on the floor laughing and yelling. Paint was spilled on both the kitchen and living room floors.

I froze. I hate them, I thought. I ran to the kitchen, took the two remaining cans of beer and emptied them down the toilet. I started crying hysterically. Philip got up and looked at me through blurry eyes.

"I tried. I'm fuckin' weak, that's all."

"Go home! Leave! Everyone leave! Get out of here!"

"Don, you're a fuckin' alcoholic! I'm a fuckin' alcoholic!" Philip was yelling at the top of his lungs.

"Leave!" I screamed. "Just leave! Get out of here!"

The two drunks dragged themselves downstairs. They yelled and laughed like lunatics, bringing neighbors out to see what the racket was all about. Mag stayed behind. She was in tears as well.

"I'll come back alone and help you tomorrow. Don't worry," she said.

When she arrived the following day, she looked upset.

Philip apologized profusely a few days after the painting party. He came to the apartment with flowers. When he took me out for dinner, I felt he was genuinely apologetic and didn't find it hard to forgive him. We hugged in the restaurant, and I felt sure he would always be my friend.

The following day, he got down on his hands and knees to strip the two wooden floors and polish them with polyurethane

"We have to talk," he said suddenly after he was done.

"Another reason I'm in therapy is…"

The doorbell rang. The pizza delivery boy handed me the pie and soda that I had ordered to celebrate the finished apartment. I carefully put the bag on the tablecloth in the middle of the gleaming, empty living room floor. As I began to open the pizza box, Philip turned to me.

"Maura, I enjoyed our time together. I'm trying to come to terms with who I really am. The problem is…" He looked away then faced me again. "I wish you every luck in your new apartment and your new life." He was packing the tools he had left under the sink. "I must tell you I'm the kind of guy you don't need. I'm too confused. You're leaving the convent now, and you're ready for a relationship. I'm not the guy." He closed the toolbox. "I hope you'll understand. I'm going to have to say goodbye."

I watched him snap the little latch on the toolbox and felt a profound sadness as he held out his arms and we hugged goodbye.

"I'll miss you. Who's going to help me with stuff?"

"Stuff?" We hugged again, both of us crying.

"The window that's stuck and stuff like that." I blinked back tears.

After he left, I sat alone on the floor, looking at the pizza and drying my eyes with paper napkins.

"This cannot be my first meal in my new apartment," I said, looking at the paper plates. "I'm not eating this."

I ran downstairs and gave the pizza to the super's family on the first floor.

"It's okay. It hasn't been touched," I told them.

For days, I felt lonely. I wondered if the loneliness would ever leave. It was strange being away from all the Sisters, fixing up the apartment by myself. My phone had been installed. I wanted to call and ask someone to come and help me. I phoned Philip and asked if we couldn't continue to be friends. I wished then that I hadn't become so attached to him. When he didn't answer, I'd put the phone down, pick it up again and redial in case I had made a mistake. I drove away the loneliness by forcing myself to focus more on fixing up the apartment.

Before I knew it, my exclostration year was coming to an end. My dispensation from Rome would soon arrive. ᘛ

CHAPTER 31

Mag Waves Goodbye

*I*N TUAM CATHEDRAL that year, my youngest brother, John, was ordained to the priesthood. It was a wonderful occasion and a great distraction for me. I looked forward to seeing my family. We rented a house in Aghamore for a couple of weeks. Though it was a cozy cottage with a front garden, the fact that we were in someone else's house bothered me.

Although I had no say in leasing the land or selling it to the neighbors after Dad's death, I gave my opinion, saying I wished Mam would have stayed at home instead of moving to London.

"You're only thinking of yourself," Mag said. She was right. I wanted to have a place in Mayo to call home. Although it must have been an enormous change for her, Mam seemed settled with the idea of staying in London, though she did keep the gray house and surrounding garden in her own name.

On this occasion of John's ordination, it wasn't the house that was on Mam's mind.

"God love him. He'll make a fine priest," she boasted to the neighbors. "I'll have one of me own to give me the last rites when me time is up."

But if she was proud of her youngest, she was embarrassed when anyone mentioned her other two sons. Neither P.J. nor Tommie was able to get on a plane or a ferry to join us.

"The devil fire the drink anyway," she said, her shoulders drooping. "It'll take them before their time." A distant, wistful look would darken her warm hazel eyes whenever P.J. or Tommie's names were mentioned.

After we settled in the rented house, Don tried to fix the leg of a little wooden table in the hallway. It fell apart when he rested his golf clubs on it. Mag, with a cup of tea in hand, rested on a chair nearby. As I passed them, carrying turf from the shed to add to the fire, I heard her say something about being buried in the local graveyard. Suddenly, Don jumped to his feet and stared at her.

"Why are you saying such a thing? Are you crazy or something?"

Mag repeated the request. "When I die, I want to be buried here in Aghamore."

She had a determined look in her eyes when she slowly rose from the chair and headed for the front room. I followed her slow steps to the fireside and dropped the basket of turf by the hearth.

"Sit here in the armchair, Mag. I heard what you just said to Don. Why in the world...?"

"Don isn't taking me seriously," she said looking at me. Her eyes, so like Mam's, were pleading and mournful. "Will you remind him that I want to be buried here in Aghamore?"

"Oh, Mag, it must be your medication that's making you talk about dying. You're too young to be going on about where you want to be buried."

Slowly, she picked her way between the suitcases that she and Don had packed, ready to take them to Shannon Airport the following morning.

"I need to rest," she whispered, and she left me with my mouth hanging open as I tried to rekindle the fire.

"The pills, I guess," Don said. "I think they're doing a number on her brain. We'll go to the doctor the minute we get back and see if the medication is too strong. She'll be okay. When we go back to New York, she'll see the doctor. The weather will be better than here, and, hopefully he'll take her off some of those pills."

Don seems positive, I thought. But I felt like a lump of coal had made its way from the brass-colored bucket by the hearth and settled in my gut. What was going on with her?

In the morning, Mag and Don waved as they pulled away from the rented house. We were all outside, wishing them a safe trip back to New York. Mag looked pale and tired, but she continued to wave and wave.

The following day, I took a bus to Galway, where I joined a six-week Irish language course in the remote area of *An Ceathrú Rúa* in the *Connemara Gaeltacht* (Irish-speaking region). I'd been looking forward to this since the beginning of my leave of absence—almost a year now. When Mam sold the land and gave all six of us a share, I knew I would use mine to study in the Gaeltacht. As I was on a leave of absence, I didn't have to hand the money over to the community. So, when the Irish Arts Center in Manhattan asked me to teach an Irish language class, I happily agreed.

At the end of my fourth week in the Gaeltacht, Peadar Mac Ionamaire, the director, was reviewing the conditional mode. He asked me, "*Dá mbeadh mile dollars agat a Mhaire, céard a dhéanfá?*"

"Well, I couldn't imagine having a million dollars, but if I did, I'd stay in Connemara for much longer than six weeks," I responded.

A knock on the door interrupted the class. Peadar beckoned me with an upward nod of his head.

"*A Mhaire, tá do chol cheathrar anseo. Is mian léi labhairt leat.*"

Why in the world would my cousin be here? Why would she want to speak with me? She knows I'm in the middle of a course. I turned off my tape recorder and headed for the door. Áine looked very troubled. She took my arm and led me outside the door. I noticed that beyond the stream dark clouds hung over Ros a Mhíl. It seemed like it was going to rain any minute.

"You look upset, Áine. What's wrong?"

"I have bad news."

"Bad news? What bad news?"

She took a deep breath and started opening and closing the

246 · Maura Mulligan

clasp of her handbag. She put her hand in and pulled out what looked to be a telegram. Then she put it back in again.

"You'll have to leave the course," she blurted.

Huge raindrops started to fall. We moved back into the hallway that led to the classroom.

Áine put her arm around my shoulders.

"You'll have to leave the course, Maura. I'm sorry to have to tell you this."

"Tell me what?" I was tense now, thinking that maybe Mam had fallen sick.

"It's Mag."

"Mag? She's on a lot of medication. She's in the hospital again?"

"No. Not this time. She's gone."

"Gone? What do you mean gone?"

"I'm sorry," she said again while tightening her arm around my shoulder.

I broke away from her embrace in horror. Thrown into a heavy gray fog, I didn't know which way to turn. I felt helpless to move in any direction.

Áine helped me collect my things from the classroom. With her assistance, I managed to go back to the bed-and-breakfast and pack my clothes. She drove me to Shannon and waited until I caught the next plane for Kennedy.

As the green patches were shrinking far below the plane's window, the peaceful grazing cows and sheep grew smaller. I was relieved that I could still notice life.

At Kennedy airport, I couldn't find my bag. I left it wherever it was and took a taxi to Gleason's Funeral Home in the Bronx. ෴

CHAPTER 32

SUPERSTITION

I T WAS SHOCKING BEYOND WORDS to see
Mag lying in her coffin. She wore the lime green
chiffon dress she'd bought in Macy's for her thirty-
fifth birthday two years earlier.

She'd looked glamorous then in her suede sandals and the gold
earrings that Don had bought her for her birthday.

The lightness of the chiffon was now in stark contrast to the
mortician's heavy hand. Kneeling there beside her coffin, I felt the
numbness leave, and my mind floated to a buried memory.

A few days following John's ordination, Mam was with me in
Galway. I was in search of tapes and books to get myself geared
up for my course. Mam's spirits were still high as she prattled
on about how having a son in the priesthood was a sure road to
Heaven. We sat on a bench in Eyre Square, enjoying the break
from the rain. People closed their umbrellas as the square became
crowded. Suddenly, Mam stopped chattering.

"Mind that tinker woman. She's coming in our direction,"
she whispered, nodding her head sideways in the direction of
an approaching woman wearing a ragged brown shawl over her
shoulders.

I hushed her. "We're supposed to say travelers, not tinkers."

"Travelers, me arse," she said in a hushed voice. "Sure that's a lot of foolishness. Everyone is a traveler of one sort or another. They're tinkers. That's what they are. Isn't it many a tin can and saucepan they fixed for me, for God's sake?"

The woman coming towards us stopped several feet away, shouting at a little boy to "Sing louder. They'll pass by and not give us anything at all if you don't sing louder."

The boy took a deep breath. "Low lie the fields of Athenry, where once we watched the small free birds fly."

Free? Where's the free? He was about seven. He wore a light, rain-soaked shirt and corduroy pants with his knees coming through. The words "free" and "fly" were flung from his tiny lungs. I felt sorry for the child, angry with the mother—if, indeed, she was his mother. She left him and walked towards me. I had one eye on her and the other on the statue of the *seanchaí*, Pádraig Ó Conaire. He sat on his stone bench behind me, an open book in his stone hand. Mam, sitting on a nearby wooden bench, took out her rosary. Fingering the beads, she pretended to ignore the woman who held a cup out to me.

"Give me a few coppers in the honor a God, and I'll say a prayer for you." The woman's eyes were demanding, darting from me to Mam. Something came over me, a combination of anger for the fate of the child and fear because of the threatening look in the woman's green eyes. I looked at the little singer and then back at the woman.

"Go away," I started. "You shouldn't have the child singing like that. He's tired and wet from the rain." I pretended to be assertive, but my voice betrayed me.

Perhaps sensing my weakness, the woman straightened up, pulled her shawl closer around her shoulders and placed both her hands a few inches away from my face, palms facing me. I moved back. She followed. I moved again. My back was against the statue now. I had the book *An Chead Cloch* that I had just bought at Kennys Bookshop. I held the book in front of my face.

The woman grabbed the book and put it in her basket. Tourists gathered around, taking pictures. I was mortified when the woman began to speak.

"My curse on you and yours." She looked at Mam when she said the word "yours." Mam rooted in her bag for a coin. She fumbled, found one, got up and threw it into the cup on the ground near the boy. The traveler was not done with me. She lifted her chin, curled her lips and continued speaking. "That no one belonging to you may live long enough to see their children's children!"

She backed away from me a few steps, turned around, and signaled for the boy to follow her. They shuffled off across the green. Mam looked up from her beads. "Now we have to go into a church," she whispered anxiously. I could hear the woman's voice coming across the lawn, demanding that the boy "sing again."

"Let's just get out of here," I moaned.

"When a red-headed tinker puts a curse on you, it's bad luck, so it is. I never met a tinker the like o' that rap, so I didn't. Come on, we'll go and get holy water at the cathedral," Mam urged.

"You go ahead. I'll stay here and wait for you." I was trying to slow my breathing. I could hear the boy's small voice as he started up the same song again.

That day in Galway, I had told Mam not to believe in superstitions. Looking at Mag in the coffin, I wished I had been nicer to the tinker. ☙

CHAPTER 33

RETURN TO THE WORLD

HILE MAG LAY IN HER COFFIN in the Bronx, Tommie lay in a hospital in London. He would not recover from alcohol poisoning.

"The ways of God are not our ways," Mam said. In spite of losing two adult children within a month of each other, her faith brought her through her grief. Though she could not bring herself to attend their funerals, she truly believed her children were better off and that their departure from this world was God's plan. She would mourn for another sixteen years and, before her own death, experience the pain of watching P.J. lose his battle with alcohol as well.

"And you, A Grá," she said. "You have a secure life married to the Lord. Are you sure you want to give it up and come back to the miseries of the world?"

"I'll probably never get over losing them—especially Mag. I knew her better than Tommie. But the convent is not the place to hide from the troubles of life."

"Ah sure, Lord God, now you're talking like the nuns in *The Sound of Music*. I mind that's what they said to Julie Andrews." We laughed, and then cried together.

"We have to find things to laugh about," she said. "We were put in this world to make the best of it."

"Well," I said, "even though I spent all those years trying to connect with God, my faith isn't nearly as deep or as trusting as yours. But I want to dance again, and leaving that secure life is my next step."

She smiled then and broke into humming a song.

"Where did you hear that?" I said, recognizing the old Shaker tune, "Lord of the Dance."

"'Twas on the radio this morning. I always thought you weren't finished dancing," she mused quietly, handing me a cup of tea.

Back in my apartment, as I took pen in hand to sign the dispensation from Rome, I heard her familiar voice in my head: "Lord between us all harm, do you feel sure you're taking the right step?"

"I do," I said. ∽

EPILOGUE

$\mathcal{I}$N THE EIGHTIES, WHEN I PERFORMED as dancer/actor at the Irish Arts Center in Manhattan, I realized the creativity that was trapped in me was finally free to fly. I founded and directed an Irish language school, *An Scoil Gaeilge*. My classes, held at the American Irish Historical Society, drew the attention of national television when Roz Abrams' "New York Views" and Jim Ryan's "Good Day New York" came to call.

The education I began in the convent led to a master of arts in education, which qualified me to teach in the New York public schools. Once there, I started a children's dance class composed of students with names like Juana, Maria, Fernando, and José. I took my steppers to perform at New York's City Hall in March (Irish Heritage Month), and they appeared on Nickelodeon with Jean Butler and Colin Dunne of "Riverdance."

In the spring of 2011, I was proud to donate my McNiff dancing costume for the exhibit "Ireland America: The Ties That Bind" at the New York Public Library for the Performing Arts. When I delivered my dress to the exhibit's curator, Dr. Marion Casey of Glucksman Ireland House at NYU, I thought of how I hadn't expected to ever wear it again after entering the convent. But I had indeed worn it when performing with my céilí dance students at New York's Abigail Adams Smith Museum, the Brooklyn Botanic Garden, and elsewhere.

My mother, in her attempt to go with the flow of my new life, wrote to me shortly after I left, saying she hoped I'd find "a nice class of a man," one that would make me happy. What a switch, I thought. She even reminded me that a leap year was approaching in case I wanted to make the first move. I told her that, although I hadn't given up my search for Mr. Wonderful, the two marriage proposals I'd turned down made me doubt my ability to commit to married life—even when the groom's name was Jesus. "Still, you never know," I added.

Through the years, I've enjoyed many wonderful visits to Ireland. These were usually sprinkled with dance and writing workshops. I even stayed for several months one winter to decide if I wanted to spend my retirement years in the land of my birth. I considered remodeling the old house, but ran into misunderstandings with a neighbor who it seems was entitled to its ownership. When my students in New York wrote asking when I was "coming home," they helped me realize that home isn't necessarily the place where you were born.

As I grew in spiritual and emotional awareness, I learned that I didn't need to attend a church or a service to pray. During my writer's residence in the Heinrich Böll cottage on Achill Island, I felt as I have often felt in this West of Ireland landscape—that nature gives me the most tangible concept of God.

On a recent visit to Achill, the early morning view of Sliabh Mór overlooking the Atlantic moved me to grab my laptop and send this e-mail to my friends and students in New York:

Subject: Sliabh Mór In The Early Morning

The mist crawls upward like a giant creature, climbing until the peak is shrouded.

Another look and the mountain has faded from sight.

As the sun rises, the cliffs are suddenly visible again.

Purple and green circles of heather and grass push through the gray mist.

The fog climbs to the summit dissolving into the cloudless sky.

Closer by, the song of a sparrow, the first sound of the morning breaks the silence.

The bird hops among the dew-drenched hydrangeas.

Blooms of pink and lavender burst from bushes of wild roses.

Beyond, the tall pampas waves regally in the early breeze.

Further away, only the wave closest to the shore seems to move.

Slíabh Mór has faded again.

I will wait here at the window, watching the morning unfold.

I wonder will the mountain return before the lark wakes the day.

꙳

HOW PLEASED I WAS: My dance costume still fit after years of being locked away.

GLOSSARY OF IRISH TERMS

a ghrá/a stór: my beloved/my darling

amadán: fool

bóthairín: small road

Ceathrú Rúa: place name in Connemara
(anglicized as Carroroe)

céilí: Irish folk dance

ciseán: basket

ciúinas: silence

cóta mór: overcoat

coillte: (wood) derogatory term for person from the country

Connemara Gaeltacht: Irish-speaking region in Galway

créatúr: creature

feadóg: a tin whistle

feis: cultural festival with competitions in dance and other arts

fear bréaga: scarecrow

gansaí: sweater or cardigan

ghillie: soft dance shoe similar to a ballet shoe

go raibh maith agat: thank you

le cúnamh Dé: with the help of God

míle buíochas: a million thanks

muise: indeed

púca: shape-shifting goblin connected with Samhain

Samhain: a Celtic harvest festival held on
October 31–November 1

scaltán: baby bird

sióg: faery, fairy

slán: goodbye

slán agus beannacht a stór: goodbye and blessings
to you, my beloved

the sidhe: the faeries, fairies

About the Author:

*M*AURA MULLIGAN WAS BORN in County Mayo, Ireland, where she worked on the family farm, danced on the stage, and served pints in a bar. In America, she became a telephone operator, then answered a higher call to become a nun. After leaving religious life, she  worked as an Irish language and dance instructor and appeared on stage as dancer and actor. A teacher of English to speakers of other languages in New York public schools, she later served as Field Supervisor in the TESOL program for Hunter College.

Her writing has appeared in the *Irish Times, Irish America, The Irish Echo, Irish Examiner, Set Dancing News, Glór Achadh Mór,* and the literary websites Ducts.org and Mr. Beller's Neighborhood. Currently, she teaches *Ceílí* dance in New York City. A firm believer that it's never too late to try on a new hat, she is working on a novel.

Lightning Source UK Ltd.
Milton Keynes UK
UKOW050818010612

193753UK00001B/4/P